I was literally born in Hope—Hope, Arkansas. But I was also raised in Hope, and not just geographically. I have lived life believing that God's "batteries" for charging our lives with the energy to keep going, no matter what we face, is HOPE. Gail McWilliams may not have been born in the same hometown, but her life is hope-filled. She has contagious optimism and joy. When I interviewed her on my show on Fox TV she talked about hope and how it always sees. I told her after the show that I think that is the title of her new book. Thank goodness she wrote *Hope Sees* ! Gail reminds us that there is no such place as hopeless. I know you will love and be blessed by this amazing book about Hope.

> —Mike Huckabee
> Former Governor of Arkansas
> Television Host

Trials in life can often lead to questions and doubts about life, faith, and ultimately God's plan for our life. In the midst of these times, what we need more than anything is hope. There is no one better to communicate this message than Gail McWilliams. Her story, combined with biblical insight, will inspire anyone in need of encouragement to persevere despite the hardships they may face. Gail is a living testimony to the truths she writes about in this book. *Hope Sees...Beyond Obstacles, Challenges and Disappointments* will move you to take confidence and believe that your best days are ahead.

> —Dr. Jack Graham
> Pastor, Prestonwood Baptist Church

If the trials of life have left you with unclear vision, then you need to see through Gail's eyes. Although blindness darkened her physical sight, her *vision* is 20/20. She shines hope into every situation...and helps us see how to live a hope-filled life —with vision for the future.

> —June Hunt
> Founder, CSO (Chief Servant Officer)
> Hope For The Heart

Gail McWilliams' life has been a journey from darkness to hope. Her ability to communicate her message of hope makes it a joy to read her words and listen to her message. Lives will be changed by *Hope Sees.*

> —Ken Davis
> Author, Speaker, Communicator

Gail delivers the amazing gift of hope. This book will not just change your perspective but possibly YOUR LIFE! Gail is the "Life Example" that *HOPE SEES.*

> —Kathy Hayes
> Co-founder, Covenant Church

My reaction when Gail speaks is a combination of laughing, crying, guilt for allowing anything to get me down, and the sense of encouragement when Gail picks up the pieces at the end of her presentation. Because of her joyful transparency, she is able to unmask each person's emotions and bring them "hope" as a reality, rather than a distant concept. Reading Gail's book will encourage you and make your life better.

> —Rabbi Steve Weiler
> Shoresh David Messianic Synagogue

We speak of hope often in whispers, as if the resolute voicing of the term will somehow make it disappear as quickly as it appeared. But Gail McWilliams knows hope and how tangible, visible, substantial and palpable it really is. She brings her friends (as I have had the privilege to be) and her readers to this understanding. If you need a clearer picture of Hope, take the journey with Gail – you will never see Hope the same!

—Camella J. Binkley
Franchise Owner, Express Employee
Professionals
Co-Founder, New Name Society
Trustee, Oral Roberts University

Her writing and speaking leave all who hear her with new hope to discover life's purposes for their lives. *Hope Sees* will take us all into new heights of challenge and expectation. It is a "must" for all to read.

—Bill Ligon
Founder of "The Father's Blessing"

Gail McWilliams' own personal story helps one to understand that there is always hope beyond all struggles. Her message inspires me to know that, when the storms of life come, hope is my anchor. Gail brings an outstanding message that lifts you up through her humorous personal stories, her insights and encouragements to look beyond the circumstances, and, as she says, to see beyond the horizon. Gail helps us to see hope as a verb and to expect with confidence that hope sees, hope gives, hope lives. A must read!

—Angie Hammond
Former Executive Director, Hope Mansion
Consultant and Trainer

Gail McWilliams is one of the most inspirational, encouraging individuals I know! Mentored by Zig Ziglar, tested by circumstance and inspired by Jesus, Gail's enthusiasm for life is infectious, and it comes through loud and clear in this latest book, *Hope Sees*. It is powerful and life changing. Thank you, Gail, for seeing what most of us miss!

—Rich Bott
President and CEO
Bott Radio Network

Gail McWilliams is truly inspirational and wise. There is a light within her that shines on everyone around her, and she helps readers see life through her eyes. She will challenge you to see hope like you never have before.

—Matt Bridges
Owner Operator, Chick-Fil-A

HOPE SEES

HOPE SEES

Beyond Obstacles, Challenges and Disappointments

GAIL MCWILLIAMS

Manufactured in the United States of America

Published by
Generations Global Press
www.GenerationsGlobal.com
"…beyond the horizon, around the globe, and to generations yet to
    come."

For information, please contact:
www.GailMcWilliams.com

Hardcover ISBN: 978-0-9906707-7-3
Ebook for Kindle ISBN: 978-0-9906707-8-0
LCCN: 2016905196

TABLE OF CONTENTS

BEFORE YOU BEGIN...

W hen I first met Gail McWilliams, we were sitting together in a small coffee shop in a large convention hotel. Crowds of people were buzzing by, and noisy conversations filled the room around us. It would have been a distraction for most people, but not my new friend. She gave me her undivided attention. After a while, I felt as though we were the only ones in the busy hotel.

I wondered if it were because she was blind, and not able to see the scores of people rushing by. Then I realized Gail was seeing something different. Something that helped her focus in a most unusual way: She was seeing into my heart. And *that* has made all the difference in our friendship.

Not many people look at life as Gail McWilliams does. The Bible says we should, though. One of the most powerful scriptures dealing with "sight" and our need to see things from God's point of view is Hebrews 11:1, "Now faith is being sure of what we hope for and certain of what we do not see."

According to this verse, faith is a sort of substitute for sight and possession. Faith is able to make invisible things appear very visible; that is, spiritual concepts that previously we couldn't see, suddenly become rock-solid real through faith. Spiritual realities that used to seem invisible become concrete and tangible. We look around us and—oh, my goodness—we can "see" what God is doing!

But faith also makes us look differently at the visible world all around us. Through the eyes of faith, the concrete world— the stuff we handle and touch and buy—no longer possesses the glow of excitement. It seems drained of substance and importance when we look at our everyday surroundings with eyes of faith.

Many Christians never achieve this level of sight. For them, all they can see are the problems and physical hardships—they do not have the ability to see these challenges from God's perspective.

But Gail McWilliams is different. Think of her as our Annie Sullivan, and we, as Helen Keller. *But wait a minute,* you say, *Gail is the one who is blind, not me!* Well, this is why the book you hold in your hands is so important. Through it, Gail, our blind guide, will draw back the veil that clouds our spiritual sight so that we might see heavenly realities come into clear focus. It's as Helen Keller wisely said, "The only thing worse than being blind is having sight but no vision."

Gail's faith in Christ is robust and rigorous. As we closed our time together in that coffee shop, she said, "Joni, I just do *not* understand bored people with excuses for everything. Life is too short and there is much to do. God is good and His grace and joy our adornment. I am driven by purpose and each day is a gift."

Would you like to be certain of spiritual realities and truths that presently you cannot see? Then carve out time each day with Gail McWilliams in this extraordinary book *Hope Sees*. For when you do, you will be able to see life as she does, recognizing that God is a God of love who is constantly working through our hurt and hardships to bless us with His joy, love, and peace.

—Joni Eareckson Tada
Joni and Friends International Disability Center

CHAPTER ONE

HOPE

*Hope is essential to living an
exceptional life on every level.*

Hope is one of my favorite topics. In my daily life hope sees around obstacles and challenges. Hope sees beyond my foggy thoughts and powerfully penetrates the anguish of any devastating news that comes my way. Hope is the wide-angle lens through which I can clearly refocus to once again see the big picture when life's urgencies and emergencies have blindsided me. Hope is visionary and sees beyond the crises of my life. Hope sees the best in every situation I face. Hope is a floodlight and shows a way for my dreams to be rescued and offers a way for my heart and soul to escape offense. Hope always sees a better way. Hope lays out an alternate course when I have lost mine. Hope sees the beginning and the end, and loves to confront the mess in the middle. When life obscures your view like a fence that stands at eye level, hope gives you a boost and places you on your tiptoes only to discover *there is more!*

Hope has been defined as the anchor of the soul. This silent life partner enables us to ride out the storms of life and make calculated adjustments when the rising tides of change threaten to throw us off course. Hope is not dependent on logic or facts, but skillfully hoists its sails in the midst of threatening winds that surround us, helping us to safely navigate the open sea of possibilities where the sky's the limit. Hope freely calls to each of us, but it can be drowned out by the cares and worries of life.

Hope is especially resilient when coupled with faith. Hope changes the first three letters of dis-appointment to *His*-appointment, reminding you to look up. In fact, this dynamic duo lifts you from the sinkholes of life to a mountaintop view of all that lies at your disposal. Hope enlarges your perspective by lighting a candle in your darkest hour. Hope keeps on singing when you thought you lost the tune. Hope remains when all have walked out of your life. Hope lives on when you think you cannot continue. Hope resides deep in the heart causing you to get back up when you've been knocked down. When you are plagued with doubts about your own abilities and strengths, hope encourages you by cheerfully reminding, "You can do this!"

Let me propose to you that hope is actually quite substantial in nature and pulsates with possibility. Hope is the mortar that holds together the building stones of your life message. Hope has infinite value when consistently attached to your deepest desires and grandest visions. Hope is the original renewable resource! Hope continually and perpetually makes itself available to all who choose it.

Hope bids us to mount up confidently on life's balance beam where it provides abilities to juggle the realities of good and bad news. The temptation to marginalize its worth or patronize its purpose *must* be resisted.

Hope longs to be your best friend. Hope is tenacious, deliberate, and constant. Hope never gives up. Hope is eternal. Hope has companions that help lift your spirit and give purpose to your life. Hope is available to all no matter their age, education, or career field. Hope helps you smile through a blur of tears. Hope instinctually sorts through the debris of your failures and hands you tools and resources to rebuild your dreams. Hope has an infinite capacity to renew, restore, and *redeem* all situations.

Hope gives you the first glimpse of your true potential in each situation. When you walk through the door with your outlook clothed in hope, the very atmosphere in a room will change. And, your changed attitude is all the catalyst you'll need to connect to a change in your circumstance. Hope is the perfect vehicle to drive your God-given creativity, skills, and vision to your desired destination.

Perhaps life has hardened your sensibilities to the point of making you a true skeptic. It's no wonder. Leaders throughout history have succumbed to the temptation of manipulating the masses by instilling within their hearts the notion of hope for political expediency or sheer popularity. But campaign slogans and buzz words are easily exposed as mere imposters of hope. If, in the past, you put your hope in the wrong person or business scheme, don't let that bad experience rob you of exploring this vital dynamic of hope.

I believe hope is essential to living an exceptional life on every level—personally, relationally, professionally, and spiritually. Hope is the stepping-stone to the positive changes we long for. But, I might ask, change from what? Is it really our circumstances that need changing or is it our mindset? What if you could find hope in the midst of the current circumstance that threatens to discourage and deflate you?

In all these ways, hope can easily eclipse both wishful thinking and wistful daydreaming.

So, take my hand and walk with me as, together, we imagine all of what hope sees.

CHAPTER TWO

SURGEON

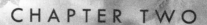

*When the white noise of your fears
and anxieties drown out hope, it
softly whispers, "Don't give up!"*

Hope is a choice. When you face the worst of conditions and wonder how you will endure life's storms, hope enables you to spot blue skies up ahead.

When I was a teen, a doctor told me I would never live to be thirty, let alone have children. At the time, his report superficially rolled off my back. But, it hid away in the deepest parts of my mind only to resurface at a crossroad in my life. Those daunting words emerged from my subconscious when I fell in love and married. In light of the fact that Tony and I wanted children, a bittersweet challenge existed as we began to have our miracle family. It was rewarding, but ever so costly. Due to a childhood disease each pregnancy created a pressure on the blood vessels of my eyes and caused me to gradually lose my eyesight.

The birth order of our children spans seventeen years. First, we had three daughters, then, after a gap of nine years, we were blessed with two additional children: another daughter and then a son. I love to call our youngest two children "goodness and mercy" because I anticipate their following us all the days of our lives. Ironically, the tables have turned, and now we seem to follow *them* everywhere.

All of our children are priceless and they keep us youthful and busy. Often I am asked, "Why would you have children when the risk was so great?" I suspect that the menacing core of such a question is: "How did you choose between convenience and legacy?"

In my worldview, legacy wins every time. My greatest vision is for generations yet to come.

Hope has accompanied me through every impossible moment of my life and every troubling medical report. In those years I knew hope was much more than a wishful dream. I trained my heart and mind to never be caught without hope. I had challenges to overcome, and chief among them was my own battle with fear.

Fear is an enemy to hope. Fear caused me to doubt that I still had value when I wondered how I could ever be the wife my husband needed. Fear frequently informed me that Tony deserved better. Fear, *my* fears, constantly compared me to other moms and loved to suggest that I came up short and shortsighted. How would I ever be the mom my children needed? And for goodness sake, who would ever call on me to carpool?

Yet, with all these obstacles, our family gained traction as hope offered us firm footing on our treacherous path—we learned to work together as a *team*. I am the visionary who is passionate about life, family, and the next generation. Learning to adapt without surrendering was a constant mind game. Making memories was my daily quest and the delightful result of not letting go of hope.

Our family talked openly about my deteriorating eyesight and how to navigate through the challenges. It affected all of us profoundly yet groomed us for more than we could see. What appeared abnormal to others soon was our norm. The benefits that resulted remain to this day.

Though there were times that each of us grieved in our own way, we never gave up hope I would see again. While waiting, we each embraced any opportunity to be more sensitive to others in their trials. Consequently, to this day, none of us like complainers.

Early on we learned that tears did not negate hope nor faith. Of course, there were times when we all longed for things to be different but we made the most of it and our family discovered hidden riches in the dark hour of our lives. Blindness threatened to rob us all, but hope stood guard over our home. Our team effort helped us accomplish more than most, and advantages formed in our temperaments as a result.

Have we suffered losses along the way? Yes. Have we gained character-building resolve in the process? Absolutely. Hope was our travel companion who aided us to see beyond, no matter the storm or brilliant skies. Hope remains the anchor of our souls in an otherwise tumultuous life voyage.

I still vividly remember one horrific storm I could not avoid. After all five of our children were safely here, I had to make one of the biggest decisions of my life. Our youngest child was two at the time and Anna, our oldest, was nineteen. My doctors were convinced that we had a small window of time to help preserve what was left of the eyesight in one of my eyes. Their tests, counsel, and network of the "greatest of surgeons" presented me with a difficult choice. No one could guarantee the outcome of this intricate surgery. Yet, what if I turned down this opportunity? Would I miss a chance to have more sight? In the short term, I was taunted by my knowledge of the surgery's temporary effect where both eyes are patched for a lengthy season of recovery. I asked for thirty days to make my decision.

One night, a doctor who was a friend of the family called me and said, "Gail, what do you have to lose?" I agreed to the surgery.

Upon my retina specialist's recommendation, Tony accompanied me to one of the top eye surgeons in the nation. He was in Chicago, four hours from our home. The surgery is called a vitrectomy. After a five-hour, intricate surgery, with twelve hundred laser shots and technical challenges, it was finished. My only memory of that infamous day was unusual peace before being taken to surgery. I did not notice when I slipped into the dark place of waiting while the surgical team worked feverishly to save my sight. I do, however, vividly remember someone calling my name at some point. I faintly heard a voice bidding my return from what seemed like the deepest dark hole in the universe. The anesthesia was wearing off. I struggled to come back to consciousness.

In my groggy state of mind, I didn't notice that four strong medical assistants had filed into my room. They posted at each corner of my surgical bed. Suddenly and without explanation, I was flipped over onto my stomach. If any warning of what was about to happen was given, I had failed to hear it. I was terrified! The medical assistants had secured me between my top and bottom sheets and flipped me like a toasted cheese sandwich on a hot grill. Suddenly alert, I was sternly warned to stay in that position for twenty-one days and was ordered to not lift my head. A gas bubble had been injected into my eye, and keeping my face down allowed the bubble to float to the back of my eye to hold their intricate work in place.

I remember lying in the back of our customized van on my stomach, feeling every bump and turn along the trip home. Tony and I barely talked. Left to imagine the road ahead of us, I had one foreboding thought. How would I lie on my stomach for twenty-one days and not lift my head?

Running to meet me at the door, the children were shocked to see both eyes patched. I was then led to my chosen spot on the floor. Most of my days were spent on the carpet. I felt like the family dog in a humiliating posture. My dear friend, Maureen, brought a soft small woolen rug to help ease the rug burns forming on my face and forearms. I was only relieved slightly toward the end of the twenty-one days when my husband obtained a piece of medical equipment. It was similar to a well-padded catcher's mitt with openings to breathe where my face lay. It raised my head off the nap of the carpet. Nothing was comfortable. I had to eat my meals with my head down. A drinking straw was a welcomed tool. At night I lay on a single mattress on the floor with my head extended over the edge. Every attempt was made to cooperate with the surgeon's instructions with the hope that I would see again. Each day I told myself, "Tomorrow will be better."

That surgery in 1998 led to three *more* surgeries that year, an important non-negotiable detail about which no one had bothered to warn me. Once the journey started there was no turning back. I "hoped" each additional surgery would restore more of my sight.

Nearly a year later, I went back to the surgeon's office for my final evaluation. I was very apprehensive. The surgeon quietly tested me and then silently looked over my chart notes. We both sat in silence as he thoroughly studied his findings. It seemed an eternity passed as hope hung in the balance. Finally, and slowly, my surgeon rolled over to me, placed his hand on my knee, and gravely said, "Gail. I'm sorry. There is no hope."

That's when the dam broke and tears gushed down my face. Every tension bottled in me from that long year was released. I kept my head erect as the surgeon offered me a box of tissues. I looked in his general direction and resolutely said, "I leave this office in hope. *No one* can take my hope!"

Hope safely anchored me that day. That awful tug of war between hope and despair reminded me in many ways of the time when our firstborn daughter was gravely ill in the prenatal center in Springfield, Illinois.

Anna was born full term but with seven dire complications. Doctors offered us no hope that she would survive. Our precious baby girl was transferred from one hospital to another and actually died twice in the ambulance as she was raced between two cities. For twenty-one days Anna fought for her life. We held onto hope then, too.

One morning, while at a hotel across the street from the high-risk neonatal center, I telephoned a Christian television prayer line to ask a complete stranger to pray for Anna. Everyone I knew was already praying for us, yet I was desperate and feared we might lose her. I reached for more hope. Fumbling to find the number, I hardly waited for the prayer counselor to ask the first question. Fighting the tears, I said, "I need help. I called to ask if you could pray for our newborn, Anna. She is in critical condition." The prayer counselor first asked, "Tell me. Is there any hope?"

Stunned by the question, I snapped back, "Of course there is hope! That is why I called you!"

He backpedaled quickly and said, "Yes. Of course! I just wanted to know what the *doctors* said." I do not remember how the phone call ended, but it was over in a flash. I threw the phone across the bed. I struggled to maintain my hope, because without it there would certainly be no faith. To this point the root of my fears was based on what we were seeing. I had to know what hope sees. Invaded by despair I had nowhere to go. A hard lesson learned was in process. I reached for my Bible. It fell to Psalm 118, *"I will take refuge in God and not man."*

When the white noise of your fears and anxieties drown out hope, it softly whispers, *"Don't give up!"* Hope is enough. Hope sees beyond the failed business, lost investments, divorce or custody battle. Sometimes, hope is all you have after the diagnosis, the betrayal, the separation, the funeral, the bankruptcy, or the natural disaster.

There is no place that hope is unwilling to go. In every situation, hope reaches out to you, but you will have to choose to grasp it firmly.

CHAPTER THREE

SCHOOL DAZE

*Hope can seem risky business when
you feel disenchanted.*

When you live with any kind of disability, there are different emotions and seasons. There is denial, anger, desperation, and overwhelming disappointment. Hope has its work cut out for it.

At the end of the day, you must determine what you will do with what has been entrusted to you. There is a life to be lived. Eventually, for me, I had to decide what I would do in the middle of my changed world. In reality, the only things that were drastically altered were my own agenda and dreams. I still had value, abilities, and faith. My hope to see again has never changed, no matter the medical report. And it doesn't matter to me if it comes by some medical breakthrough or a miracle. I am ready. But, in the meantime, life goes on and I do not want to miss anything.

You may struggle to even relate to my changed world, but imagine a few things I have never seen. I have never filled my own tank of gas. When I was last driving, the service attendant filled it for me. I have never used an ATM machine, though it has braille capability. By the way, I don't read braille. I have never used self-serve checkout at a grocery store. I don't know what an icon looks like on my computer screen. I've never seen the face of my iPhone. I must unfortunately depend on Siri who never seems to get my texts right.

I can't order off a menu by myself and the pictures are of no help either. I can't see to watch TV, but that is probably a blessing because I wouldn't know which remote to use or how to use the fancy technological gadgets. I have no idea what colors are in this year for my wardrobe, but my daughters are fashionable and they love to shop for me. I have no idea if a light bulb needs to be changed. I cannot understand why others have to flip the light on when they enter the room. I don't know if that's our dog in the backyard or a coyote.

I have used audio books long before they were the rage. Voice activated things are not new to me. My imagination is excellent and I am your very best friend—you look great to me every day! The list is endless of what I cannot see but hope has helped me concentrate on what I can still do. I am sure you have never seen what I see and that is the point of this book.

To adjust to my new world and its challenges I needed to learn some new skills. I surmised the biggest and most advantageous was the computer. One day I was finally ready to take on the challenge. When we moved to Texas in 2000, I discovered I was eligible to apply for some specialized computer training for the visually impaired, compliments of Texas Commission for the Blind (TCB). Since I see myself as a visionary living in a blind world, the idea of not seeing is still foreign to me. Still, I wanted to learn. I had no idea of the immense challenge this would prove to be.

Anna, our firstborn, agreed to be my companion during the classes and I was scared spitless. It seemed like just yesterday when I held *Anna's* little hand as she went to kindergarten. Now our roles were reversed. As Anna escorted me to my first day of computer class at the ripe young age of 45, nothing could have prepared me for what lay ahead!

As we entered the large room with wall-to-wall computers, I met my teacher who was also blind. All the other blind students had their service dogs as their companions—and there I stood with Anna! Standing in a room where no one could see, I wondered why I had even bothered to comb my hair! I apprehensively realized I was in for the challenge of my life.

My assignment was to learn Windows, an extremely visual computer program, yet I could not see one icon. Actually, I had lost my eyesight years before the computer had become a household item. With determination, I sat down ready to learn everything I needed to join the computer-savvy world.

Right off the bat, I was thrown a curve ball: I came to class psychologically prepared to learn *one* computer program but was quickly informed that I would be required to learn an additional program called JAWS that would communicate all information to me audibly. So, my computer screen was crowded with three cursors that integrated these two programs. Most of the computer world finds a picture on their screen and points to what they want, but not me. I had to learn the codes, hot-keys, and memorize concepts from multiple manuals.

The classes were three hours long and my brain was overwhelmed! Everyone was given a break halfway through the first class. All my classmates exited the room to walk their dogs outside for a time of refreshment and relief. I leaned over to Anna and asked if she had need of a tree or fire hydrant, but she declined my offer. I admonished her *not* to be sniffing around other's belongings while she sat and waited. We both laughed and it helped relieve some of our tension.

The first three months of class were rough, but I never gave up. I quickly advanced from a blind instructor to the only sighted teacher. Her name was Ann. Her teaching style was kinder and she gave me hope that I would, eventually, catch up to the modern world. But first, I had to find my on and off switch. Ann was vivacious and personable with a great laugh. Her love for learning made me want to excel. Ann had a degree in mechanical engineering and had taught physics for years. She worked with computers all her life, and she was an airplane pilot to boot. In addition to software training, Ann expanded my Texas vocabulary. There is NO end to the education and nuggets I learned from my favorite instructor who at the time was sixty-seven years old!

Another motivating force to not give up was my fellow student named Karen. She was in her early twenties. She had the most delightful personality and was sharp as a tack. Karen had a 3.95 GPA in chemical engineering before her life was rudely interrupted by two cancerous tumors, which attached themselves to her optic nerves in her junior year of college. On the days she was not in class with me she was at the hospital receiving chemotherapy. I was challenged on a weekly basis by one senior citizen and a new friend with two brain tumors.

The challenge of any medical set back is to fear the unknown and react to the changes of your life agenda. My short lived times of wondering, "Why me?" soon turned to, "Why not me?" Still, I have felt alone and wondered if anyone could relate to the large learning curve thrown at me while feeling blindfolded and disadvantaged. Perhaps, it was in those times of wishing things were different that I found out that hope is more than a wishful thought. My attitude and outlook changed when I decided to focus on what I had been given, rather than what I had lost. Nothing could replace or make up for the losses—there were too many. Yet, I had today and the freedom to choose what to do with it. My rugged climb intersected with some wonderful people who modeled courage and resilience to me. Determination was my companion and hope guarded my heart as I resolved to go on and live.

The computer classes were a "gift" through a non-profit organization that taps donors, grants, and even funding from the state. But to get my own computer I had to jump through many hoops. I remember where I was the day a state facilitator asked, "Why do you need a computer?" I told her I wanted to have an expansion for communication. I shared my plan to write a book of my story one day. She laughed and sarcastically said, "Oh yeah! Everyone wants to write a book someday. Now, really! What do you need a computer for?" Looking back, I am surprised I even showed up for my first computer class with a cheerleader that pessimistic. I did mention her name in my acknowledgments of the first edition of my first book, *Seeing Beyond* with, of all things, a foreword by Zig Ziglar. By then, you would have thought it was her idea that I write books.

My computer class provided me with the skills to write and eventually publish books. I knew I had finally arrived the day the computer department called me from the non-profit organization where my husband worked. They had various glitches in some of the main computers and needed to know the hotkeys for specific technology processes. I could not believe I aided the computer department with the little I knew.

Everyone has challenges. The question is what you will do with them. Some think life is too hard while others love the adventure. It is scary to show up in life without knowing what others know. You can back away or ask to learn. Life is the classroom. Nothing seemed more hopeless to me than attempting to learn advanced computer skills. I could have whined and felt sorry for myself, but instead, I wrestled weekly with my inadequacies. None of it was easy, all of it hard. Yet now, years later, I look back and see the freedom that came from taking the risk.

Hope can seem risky business when you feel disenchanted. Perhaps what you face is not your life plan. How do you reckon with a God who states, "Hope never disappoints?" Yet you have tasted disappointments. But no matter what, hope sees beyond any risk and moves you forward. You may not know the outcome, but hope meets any challenge with resolute confidence.

CHAPTER FOUR

CHICKEN CAR

*Your gift of appreciation gives
hope in a world of mundane
routines.*

I f you struggle with feelings of hopelessness, ingrati-
tude might be the real culprit sabotaging your outlook.
Developing an attitude of gratitude takes a little practice, but
soon it will become second nature to give thanks to those who
have helped you.

Giving gifts is my favorite thing to do. Obviously, I have
a few challenges to work around, but my imagination is huge
and my determination resolute. Besides, the fun is to think of
a creative way to get the job accomplished.

Years ago I lived near a kind and thoughtful friend named
Judy. She was easy to be with and laughed at my humor. An

ordinary trip always ended up with loads of fun and memories. Her kindness and generosity were gifts to me as she willingly picked me up to take me on errands. We had so much fun together that soon we added extra outings. She was always eager for an adventure, plus, she drove a great car that was comfortable and stylish. We had enjoyed so much time together and I felt indebted to her in a myriad of ways.

In the early years of my blindness I often struggled with feelings of value. And, before she met me, Judy once struggled with feelings of low self-esteem. It's still hard for me to imagine that Judy once doubted her life held much purpose. Soon, we became fast friends.

It did not take Judy long to see just how valuable she was and how I cherished her gifts of kindness. Along the way, Judy and I found other women to include in our friendship. On our frequent outings, we would often pick up one of these new companions. Some of these women struggled with depression. Before long we had our new friend laughing with us and she would leave our outings full of hope and feeling loved.

Judy's birthday was near and I wanted to surprise her with a memorable day on the town. It took some scheming to put it all together. Another friend agreed to assist me with my master plan. I called Judy several days before her birthday to see about her availability and secure the date.

"Hey Judy! This is Gail. I want to take you out to lunch on your birthday. Will you be free that afternoon?"

She readily said, "Yes." And then asked, "When should I pick you up?"

I said, "No Judy! I've got this one covered. I am picking *you* up this time. The day is on me."

She nervously laughed and said, "Okay. I can't wait!"

During those years, our family lived in Central Illinois. In our small city there was an ice cream place that had an old car for loan. It was a long, older model Cadillac. It was an effective marketing tool in our community because it sported the business name and logo in magnetic letters on each side of the car. Everyone called it the Chicken Car for a good reason. On top of the car was a five-foot tall rooster's head, and out the back trunk lid was a five-foot rooster's tail. It was hideous and its color was atrocious. I called the ice cream joint and reserved the fowl mobile. They never asked if I was blind—and I never told them.

On the day of my rental, I asked my friend Ruth to go pick it up for me. It worked best since she had a license and could see to drive the contraption to my house. From there we decorated the Chicken Car with more signs and balloons. My game plan was going perfectly.

Judy and her family lived out in the country. Ruth agreed to drive me to the edge of town. At the county line, we switched places and I was in the driver's seat. We placed a large sign on the passenger window that said something crazy about Judy's age. The sign was a convenient cover-up for my friend, Ruth, who rode low on the floor to peer over the dashboard to assist me in driving.

"Stay to the right and move slowly," were two of her first instructions. "Okay, now speed up a little," giggled my guide of steel.

With my hands on the steering wheel, I appeared to be out for a leisurely drive through the countryside. I knew my grand entrance wouldn't be lost on Judy. She was always ready early for any event. This day was no different. She sat in her dining room, looking out the bay window at the long county road to her house. Judy told me later, "I was sitting, ready to go, when I noticed something strange coming in the distance. It *looked* like the Chicken Car. I stood to my feet to get a closer look. To my shock, it *was* the Chicken Car!"

While Judy was gawking out her window, Ruth and I progressed down the way until we reached her long gravel driveway. I turned on my blinker like I was in city traffic. With courageous Ruth's help, I managed to avoid the ditch on both sides of the driveway. I slowly made the wide turn but soon sped up with zeal while I honked the horn enthusiastically and waved wildly.

Judy could not believe the clownish display before her! Colorful balloons tugged at their strings, signs were plastered on the car's windshield, and towering above all the chaos, the proud rooster announced that the party was underway!

With some fine-tuned help from my human GPS, I inched the Chicken Car closer to her garage near the side porch of her house. In the nick of time, Ruth's nervous whisper commanded, "*Stop!*" By this time, Judy had exited the side door cackling like a hen, leaning over the porch rail, laughing uncontrollably. I got out of the car and yelled from the driver's side, between the rooster's beak and the windshield, "Happy Birthday! You ready to go?"

She could not catch her breath to utter one word. I was beaming with self-satisfaction. When she finally opened the passenger door, my partner in crime rolled out onto the ground. When Judy spotted Ruth, the roar of hysterical laughter started all over again. This was a birthday none of us would ever forget.

"Judy, I brought a birthday hat for your excursion today. I want you to be 'Queen for a Day.'" Like a good sport she put it on and got in the front passenger seat. Throwing the keys to my accomplice, I announced, "Hey, Ruth, it's your turn to drive." Still laughing, everyone was relieved to have me now in the back seat.

I sat behind Judy to help point out the sites and I waved often at passing motorists who waved back at Judy. Talk about a "joy-ride." Everyone had smiles and did double takes at the crazies in the Chicken Car.

We ate at the finest restaurant by the lake. Unfortunately it didn't have valet parking, but we parked close enough for all to see our infamous limousine from the large lakeside windows. Everyone inside the restaurant looked us over when we sat down for our birthday banquet.

Afterwards, we burned up a whole tank of gas as we drove Judy to her favorite sites and shops in town. Plus, we managed to drive by her husband's corporate office building. Before going home, I suggested a treat of Judy's favorite ice cream for some icing on the proverbial cake. Of course, this was done through the drive-thru window. Halfway into the small space, we all screamed at once, "Watch out for the rooster's head!" Ruth jumped out of the car to check our clearance under the canopy. The rooster's head barely cleared the opening. Employees came to take a closer look at the celebrity limousine and its festive passengers. I just kept smiling.

Developing an attitude of gratitude takes a little practice, but soon it will become second nature to give thanks to those who have helped you. In our busy daily lives, it is easy to confuse wishful thinking with true thoughtfulness. Each of us knows a dozen little ways to instill hope in the lives of those around us and brighten someone's day. Your gift of appreciation gives hope in a world of mundane routines and overscheduled calendars.

All those countless times Judy had escorted me around town she was providing me with more than a set of wheels. Her thoughtfulness was a tangible form of hope. Without her help, I couldn't run the errands necessary in managing my household. But more than errands were at the center of our friendship. Mentoring, coaching, and heart-to-heart conversations led us both to grow. My days with Judy always left me with the sense that my visual loss was no reason to live without hope. What she could not see in her life was evident to me. What I could not do was easy for her.

Sad, lonely, and hopeless is no way to spend your life. As you wait in hope, extend hope to others and be grateful. Look back and see all the good that has happened and believe more is on the way. I am not sure how many your car holds, but pick up some friends and make a memory. Offer some joy and hope to someone and enjoy the rewards of investing in others. Warning—extending hope is contagious.

CHAPTER FIVE

REACH

You are a perfect candidate for
hope's conduit.

Tony and I have been married for nearly forty years. We have mastered the dance between a man who can see and a woman with impaired eyesight who is a visionary. Tony McWilliams exemplifies a gentleman by opening doors, holding out chairs, escorting me through life, and always being watchful for his bride. Of course, I've also told my husband, "If you'll simply offer me your arm you will look like a gentleman and I will look like your lady. Unless, of course, you walk me into a wall. Then you will look like a jerk and I will look blind." So, we've assumed our roles and the music plays on.

One day Tony was speaking for an event in Dallas. The large auditorium was filled to capacity, and the center aisle was long. He addressed college students with a lecture on character. Upon leaving the stage, Tony stopped by the front row where I was seated and said, here's my arm. I walked with him down the long aisle until we reached the last row of seats. There, Tony stepped over to the right side of the aisle and began to visit with people, while I stepped to the left side and did the same.

After a while, I eased my way over to the middle of the auditorium and placed my hand on his arm, indicating I was finished and ready to go. Like a lady of worth, I was swiftly escorted into the foyer and nearly out the front door when the usher whispered to me, "So, do you want to go home with your husband, or the man you're holding on to?"

It seemed I had reached for the wrong arm.

For a season I was embarrassed over that awkward moment. Everyone got a big laugh out of my mistake and I felt the brunt of it all. Truthfully, not seeing is harder than it looks. I've had to learn to laugh at myself along this pathway that seems increasingly dim. One day I was retelling this story in a presentation when I realized my perspective was skewed. What on earth was *wrong* with that man who gave me his arm and escorted me out of the building? He could see perfectly and he knew I wasn't his lady. Where was he taking me anyway? That forward man was the one who should have felt the brunt of the embarrassment, not me. He had set me up.

The same is true in our lives when we face awkward situations with embarrassing outcomes. We imagine that the world is laughing at us. It's time for a new perspective. Life may not look like what others think it does. Most people live life in fear of moving forward. Often, people come into our lives to simply move us from one point to another. Just exercise wisdom in selecting the arm you reach out for. Relationships are important but not all are beneficial. Grabbing the arm of one who can only see doom and gloom will cloud your vision. You may miss beautiful possibilities beyond all the clouds. Taking the arm of a critic will cause you to become critical. Holding the arm of one who is rude and crass will corrupt your vocabulary and erode your good manners. Linking arms with pessimists will only serve to convince you that your abilities are woefully unsuitable for your lofty dreams.

You are on the move. With whom have you aligned yourself?

A wise person will walk with others who are wise. It is important to take an honest look at who you have surrounded yourself with and where those relationships are leading you. A group of whiners usually find it hard to dream big. They only see what is wrong. You need friends who know how to dream and possess an attitude that nothing is impossible. You need true friends who see no limitations.

Some people can only see through filters of their own fears and insecurities, let alone encourage your lofty dreams. They feel threatened by any potential they sense in your life. Yet they like to hang around you and bum off your positive outlook.

And, if you've isolated yourself due to your past disappointments, you have missed the boat entirely. Take each moment in life and seize it. Live with the expectant hope that each day offers golden opportunities for personal growth and character development. When you encounter embarrassing situations—as we all do—learn to laugh at yourself and move on.

If the fear of embarrassment or the fear of failure continues to hold you back, you have underestimated the valuable lessons they can teach you. Quickly recover from your attitude that centers all focus on you alone. You may have the leading role in your life-play, but the story is still evolving and includes a supporting cast of characters. As you recover from the embarrassment of yesterday's failure and loss, don't be thrown if you still need to course-correct in order to hit your target. Believe me, I know this lesson all too well.

We had a group of people over for dinner one evening. It was great fun. After dinner we all migrated to my office to watch a special video on my computer monitor. There were enough chairs for most, but not for all, so I stood next to a tall young man who was seated. I like to encourage people and sometimes there are ways to do it without words. Catching the eye with a kind look across the room is one such way. Smiles, nods or just acknowledging people in the room is a kindness. Any of these modes of nonverbal communication work *if* you are visual, but in my world I must rely on touch.

Standing between guests, I reached over to pat the shoulder of the tall young man who sat to my right. In that one gesture, I hoped to silently say, "I see you and I care." Unfortunately, I had no idea he had stood up. My hand grasped what felt like the fattest shoulder I had ever touched. I quickly processed this startling fact as I kept reaching to find his shoulder. The more I reached, the stiffer he got. At the end of this exploration, I suddenly flushed, realizing I had just assaulted the entire backside of one of our dinner guests. I was mortified. *He* was horrified as he stood perfectly still. If I could have easily found the door, I would have run out of the room. Instead, I had to face one of my greatest fears. Looking up to the tall man, I said, "If you ever tell anyone about this…" My voice trailed off, unable to finish my empty threat. We both stood quietly with no one noticing my regrettable and embarrassing mistake. No words could convey my embarrassment that night when I missed my target and my intent to encourage. It's crazy how things can turn out in life. That tall young man is now my son-in-law!

The rest of our single children worry that I may try to find their mates the same way. Because of my memory of deep-seated embarrassment, the temptation I must continually overcome is to never reach again. I wish this was the only sorry tale of missing my reach. Embarrassing situations still happen in my life, but I am determined to keep reaching.

When you reach for anything it is risky. Many, though, have reached for a goal and missed. Target practice isn't limited to a shooting range. It is about your targeted area of effectiveness. The reason we are afraid to reach for our dreams is our fear of missing the mark. Your dashed hopes are merely the by-product of the power of fear. Inevitably, your past mistakes seek to limit your options for personal growth. The fear of failure is counter-intuitive. I marvel at those who feel they are stuck. If you think you are stuck, you will live stuck.

Life is too short to not reach for the next open door. You may be blinded to it currently, but it is because you have nurtured the notion of feeling stuck. You have options. I truly believe the passage of scripture that states, "Your gift will make a way for you." This truth alone should give anyone hope. It opens doors and connects you with divine appointments. Your gifts are as unique as your fingerprints and are yours alone. Someone is currently looking for the gifts you possess, gifts that will have a positive effect on many.

The poet, Robert Browning, once said, "Ah, but a man's reach should exceed his grasp, or what's a heaven for?" Some of the things we try to grasp slip through our hands. Yet, there is more to reach for and discover. I admire the leader who intentionally reaches out to strengthen and encourage the team. Have you noticed that the most effective leaders are multi-directional in their reach?

The best leaders reach out to those who lack experience or have fallen behind due to misjudgment. These leaders assist teammates to get back on track. Compassionate leaders reach for those who are lagging or are in desperate need of a personal mentor. Exemplary leaders reach out to those who come alongside. They eagerly check in with their peer group and, together, these leaders pattern camaraderie and encouragement. Asking the right questions and sharing solutions with others who seek them are characteristics of socially mobile individuals. Collaborating with like-minded pioneers is essential for a leader's knowledge base and sphere of influence to increase.

I have two dear friends who are Chick-fil-A business operators. Matt and Rob tell me of regular meetings where other Chick-fil-A operators meet to discuss what is working for their specific location and the success they have seen in their operations. The team of leaders also problem-solve together and assist each other, though they could be competitors. I asked Matt one day, "Is it hard to share your best ideas with someone who might benefit from them and take some of your own business away?"

Matt explained the core of his company is a commitment to servant leadership. Business is all about serving people and meeting their needs. You may be on the giving side of ideas this month but in need of some new innovative ideas next month. Once more it is the true example of Zig Ziglar's formula for success: "You can have everything in life you want, if you will just help enough other people get what they want." Success breeds success. When you examine a lifestyle of servant leadership it is simply the golden rule in operation.

Progressive leaders gratefully reach forward to their own mentors. As their resumes blossom, inspired leaders are increasingly aware that they did not arrive at this juncture in their careers without the patient guidance of those who came before them. Above all, the most effective leaders are lifetime students and they never tire of learning.

Most important, a humble leader reaches up, realizing his own reach may have limitations—but there is One whose reach is unlimited. The God of Hope alone possesses the strategies, surprise connections, and favor that give fresh hope for every new day. In fact, He promises in Jeremiah 29:11, "For I know the thoughts that I think toward you, says the Lord, thoughts of peace and not of evil, to give you a future and a hope."

So, reach again.

One evening, I was seated at a banquet beside the Governor of our state. We both were guest speakers at the event. It was not the first time we had worked together, and I noticed that the Governor did not seem his warm, jovial self.

I said, "Governor, you don't seem like yourself tonight. Are you okay?"

The Governor shared, "I have had one of the most stressful weeks of my life."

By this time, the program had started and it was difficult to hear each other. As a result, I turned toward the Governor to reach toward his arm and deliver a personal word of encouragement. As I reached, my mind was suddenly flooded with my past mishaps. My momentary fear almost kept me from following my instincts, but I pushed through my apprehension and said, "Governor, thank you for your faithful service to the people of Texas." I added some other words of specific encouragement, referencing accomplishments he had made in our state. The Governor thanked me sincerely. I started to turn back to my plate and enjoy the program, when I felt prompted to add to the encouragement. Turning again, I said, "Oh, yes, Governor. There is one more thing. May the Lord bless you and keep you, the Lord make his face to shine upon you and be gracious to you; the Lord lift up his countenance upon you and give you peace."

Though the governor was there to receive an award and I was the keynote speaker, I believe the divine appointment that night was to encourage a weary leader. Hope will help you reach once more, regardless of past experiences. You are a perfect candidate as hope's conduit. Keep reaching—others need your touch.

CHAPTER SIX

UNCLE

*Hope extends its hand when
you fall.*

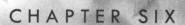

My husband has an aunt and uncle who live in Southeastern Illinois. Uncle Glen and Aunt Marilyn's farm has always been the favorite spot for Tony and his cousins to congregate. Life there is FUN. Everything is surrounded by fields as far as you can see, with haylofts to jump out of and motorized adventures on golf carts and four-wheelers. And, the meals at Aunt Marilyn's table were always the best. This was due in large part to freshly butchered hogs and cows. At first, these farm animals hung in the garage, waiting to be processed into pork chops, bacon, steaks, and hamburger.

Living off the land and married to your work do not leave much room in the budget to contract professional help in areas outside of your expertise. This might have been the reason for

Glen and Marilyn's experiment in roof maintenance. They noticed a growing concern—mold. A neighbor gave them the idea that bleach might quickly remove this unwanted intruder from their gray shingles and retard the mold's spread. With nothing to lose but a little time, they decided any good idea was worth a try. Aunt Marilyn held onto the ladder for Uncle Glen as he shinnied up the rungs, never giving a single thought to his artificial hip.

"Hey Marilyn!" the seasoned farmer yelled down to his wife. "Hand me the hose, will ya?"

Experienced in working as a team, Marilyn complied, watching as her hubby covered a large section of the roof with the liquid bleach. "Be careful up there!" came her stern command. Hoping this scheme would work, Marilyn became distracted as she calculated how much bleach she would need to buy to complete the job when she went to town the next day.

But, as Uncle Glen reached the roof peak, the elderly farmer stepped onto the ride of his life. The man-made ski slope was open and the skiing was unhindered. The silky bleach had enhanced the slippery mold on the roof and there was no bannister to grab. With his arms flailing, Glen danced a jig as he desperately tried to stop his momentum. Glen yelped and wheezed as he slid down the bleach covered, makeshift, ski slope. Even the gutter was no help in slowing him down before the sudden drop to the hard ground—without the benefit of a snowy cushion to soften his fall.

Stunned, Aunt Marilyn watched in horror as she ran to where her life partner lay face down on the ground, completely silent and stiff as a board. Finally, she was relieved to hear a low moan and the faint soft directive, "Go get my crutches."

That action-filled scene would live in their memory long afterwards. Their failed attempt to kill the roof mold landed Uncle Glen in the hospital, following the ambulance ride. Later, from his wheelchair with a broken pelvis, he convincingly advised others to hire out their roof jobs to experts.

As with any ambitious goal, the climb to the top is often exhilarating. The resume of your life experience is enhanced by devising strategies, maneuvering obstacles and overcoming challenges along the way. Reaching the top rung on the ladder of success as your career peaks *is* admirable. But take care! Without warning, prideful arrogance can creep in and turn your aspirations into a slippery slope. Especially when little consideration was given to the team who gave you a boost.

Propping one's self up on the pedestal of self-admiration is disingenuous. Surely, you didn't reach your goal without the aid and support of those around you. Most likely, someone offered a lift to your lofty dreams. Who opened the door for you, or recommended you for the place that became a stepping-stone to your coveted position? Your ideas might have been brilliant, but certain aspects of your achievement took teamwork. Even if the least among your colleagues gave you one word of inspiration or a nugget you added to your masterpiece, you owe them a debt of gratitude or a simple word of thanks. Your climb represents rungs of seasons, experiences, opportunities and learned skills. Your success, hopefully, is more than a narrow peak but is a solid platform from which you can impart hope to others who seek to duplicate your proven success.

What about looking back to embrace those you left behind? Do you ever think of them? Many who aggressively climb the ladder of success have little regard for those they pass along the way. Using people and caring only for your own self-centered ambitions tend to distract you from those valuable people you meet. Once at the top of your own ambitions, do you find yourself waving with no one noticing? Being alone as you climb can have reasonable consequences, compared to being successful and applauded by your peers. Perhaps, you are your own main obstacle! Consequently, the loss of your footing in your career, marriage, or studies is due to your self-based preoccupation.

Is there hope after a fall? What once seemed sure may now be uncertain after falling on your face or experiencing disappointing outcomes. Assess the damage to your dream and your ego and then get back up. As long as you have breath, there remain lessons to learn. You may need some time to mend, but don't take too long. Like muscles that are not used, atrophy sets in and your strength weakens. Work through your pain and hope for a new day. It will come.

Why is it when we lose our grip we wonder who witnessed it? The commentary of co-workers or competitors can deplete you of what you need to get back up and run again. Choose to be like the Olympian who fell but got up and finished the course, though bruised and hurting. Your focus should be to finish well. Scars are trophies worn by persistent warriors who didn't grow weary in the battles of life. Wear them with humility and honor.

Years ago, friends of mine coauthored their first book. They found a niche that few had written on and their book was projected to be a marketable success. A publishing company arranged to meet with them over lunch to talk about the details of the possible contract.

No book deal has ever fallen on its face quite like this one. They dressed professionally for the lunch meeting. Tom wore his best suit and Adrian wore a blouse and blazer as the perfect paring to her mid-calf, flowing skirt and high heels. The restaurant had terraced seating with different tiers of dining. Their luncheon host was already seated and watched the handsome couple approach the table. Adrian led the way up the short flight of three steps with Tom right on her heels—literally. As Adrian cleared the second step, Tom inadvertently stepped on her skirt. Their elegant processional was plagued by the domino effect that resulted in a surprise pile up. First, Tom knocked Adrian flat onto her face and then he fell on top of her! Lifting his head, he looked at the future business partners and said, "Hi. My name is Tom and this is my wife Adrian."

Talk about a good first impression. With some help and hope of a chance to start the luncheon over, the couple found their seats and thankfully stayed in them the entire lunch. Hope extends its hand when you fall and compels you to get back up. Laughter is good medicine, too. Joy and hope often work together. Learn to laugh at yourself.

Pride hates vulnerability and wears itself out trying to be perfect. A heightened sense of vulnerability is the unwelcomed side effect of any fall, but don't let your temporary clumsiness distract you from the real goal you hope to accomplish. Like a loving parent encourages their toddler after each fall, we must tell ourselves to brush it off and get up and try again.

Tears often accompany a fall, but I have learned that tears do not disavow hope. The fall of a leader is notably worth crying over. When leaders fail or fall, many lives are adversely affected. Too often, fallen leaders are encouraged by their handlers to go right on living like nothing happened. Hope helps you partner with grace to ask forgiveness and seek out restoration. Humbly face those who were disappointed or led astray by your poor judgment or lack of wisdom. You can help others learn from your mistake while you model to others a changed life. When lying flat on the floor, the biggest test of all is deciding to get back up!

The more serious, sometimes fatal fall, is to fall into despair. Falling into self-pity is a slippery slope with no one to catch you. The wise counsel that warns, "pride goes before a fall" will help you to pace yourself. Don't fall for the lie that there is no hope. Get back up and face the potential of the day.

One afternoon, back when we only had three children, we went on an autumn outing. Anna was 8, Lindey, 5 and Holly, 3. Near our home there was a two-story, outdoor children's slide on private property in a wooded area. It wasn't just extra tall; it was long and curved at several spots as well. We brought waxed paper on our excursion to make the slide even slicker. For hours the girls climbed up the rungs of the tall ladder, slid down the long extended slide and then ran back to do it all over again. Tony stood at the bottom of the ladder to give each of our little ladies a boost. It was fun to hear the girls squeal with laughter each time they came down the well-polished slide. They loved it.

A couple hours passed and our youngest, Holly, suffered a mishap. After successfully climbing to the top, Holly unexpectedly turned around to look down at her Dad. Without warning, she lost her grip and plunged into a free fall from two stories up. Amazingly, Tony was alert and caught her perfectly. No scrapes, bruises or broken limbs—just an incredible catch and two badly shaken parents.

I wish all falls had such safe, happy endings. Hope offers a safety net that will keep you from other hazards, if only you will enlist its help. Isn't it time to fall into the open arms of hope?

CHAPTER SEVEN

EMPTY

*Hope has the uncanny ability
to appear in the most hopeless
moment.*

One season I have clearly dreaded is the very one some of my friends have longed to see. It is the empty nest season. It is sad to think that our children leave our homey nest when they are finally potty-trained and well-mannered and can actually carry on great conversations. All of that work of raising them just to land in a nest of their own making, enhanced by their own gifts, skills and career path, feels bittersweet to me. But I would not want it any other way. I enjoy seeing my children spread their wings and soar to new heights beyond the place from which we launched them. I am not fully sure who sets the exhausting pace of the family treadmill.

Consider all the endless nights of crying babies that eventually dawn on the chaotic toddler-years with spills, messes, and loads of cute times. Personalities develop and vocabularies increase. Coloring, puzzles, and learning to read are fascinating to watch. Each precious moment is stamped in our hearts.

Then the first day of school arrives and you hug them and try to hide your tears as they leave the house, excited and scared. Each passing day serves to further prepare our children to leave our nest, and we hope they are ready. The young elementary years are crazy busy with new routines, skills, activities, growth spurts and frequent visits from the tooth fairy.

It's as if aliens abduct our sweet little children and leave book reports, science projects, and sports paraphernalia scattered throughout their bedrooms. All over again, new developments take place in their personalities and vocabulary, where new-found opinions erupt and brazen words are not so skillfully crafted to push our buttons. It's like there is a hormonal experiment going on in the family laboratory, but it's actually our preteens in disguise. One minute they hate us and the next minute they desperately need us. It is a challenge to juggle their growing independence, but, if we're honest, skills developed during this time empower their future.

Then, just when their mood swings appear to level out and you grow fond of their help in running errands for the household and fresh interchanges in relationship, off to college, trade school or boot camp they go, or perhaps into the work force or into a marriage—with lingering hugs of farewell and tears that are far harder to hide.

Where did the years go?

Frankly, the empty-nest syndrome sounds awful to me. I love the busy revolving door at my house, even if it is for a brief moment in our overbooked lives. Then, the married children bring those little grand-birds back to our nest to get the best of our time and love because we finally have parenting allegedly figured out. The reward for this hard-won accomplishment is our grown-up names of Nona and Poppa. Oh the joy of legacy and its golden potential! During these joyous times, our empty nest is disrupted and untidy for a few brief days. But, later, when the house empties and all the beds are once again perfectly made, order seems grossly overrated.

But, what if everything that has been mentioned is tragically interrupted by unexpected loss and penetrating grief? When you absolutely are convinced you cannot move on, hope holds you tightly. There are measurements of empty that only hope has the capacity to handle.

How do you handle empty?

Baby Eden's birth was due in a few weeks. This expectant joy filled her young parents' hearts as they finalized her nursery in preparation for her arrival. Then suddenly, an unexpected tragedy transpired without any notice, and Eden's little heart stopped beating. No words can describe the pain of delivering a stillborn child. Her parents' empty arms ached to hold their little Eden. Their hearts were broken as they cried endless tears in hope of making it through long days and the feeling of empty tomorrows. Hope weeps, too, yet gently assures that the future still has promise.

Jared's empty room was untouched for years after his sudden death at a rural railroad crossing. The overgrown bushes on the country road had concealed the oncoming train, and the crossing didn't have the usual warning signals or cross gates. In relative obscurity his promising young life was taken. Hope was present to absorb the shock and pain of his family and friends. Even years later hope helps sort revisited emotions.

Elizabeth's dorm room was suddenly empty when, one minute after midnight, she was killed in a rollover accident. There was no note of farewell to comfort her far-away family. Twenty years later, her life of great, untapped potential is still remembered by her family and friends who ache to hold her again in their souls' outstretched arms. Heaven's Hope is to see her again one eternal day. Family scrapbooks are empty of her pictures, but hope stills sees the beauty of her life.

Hope has the uncanny ability to miraculously appear in the most hopeless moment.

Brenda's husband loved life and had a personality to match. The community knew him as a vivacious pastor and visionary. He was innovative, creative and always positive. To his way of thinking, no dream was too big and no challenge was too hard. Everyone admired his zeal. He had recently found new in-roads of ministry and service to the residents of his city. His favorite role was to wear two hats, one as an auxiliary policeman and the other as the chaplain for the police department.

Their oldest daughter and son-in-law were in the process of moving so the grandchildren were staying over at their house. That morning they had enjoyed Poppi's special Mickey Mouse pancakes for breakfast. It was always a fun memory. Brenda rehearsed for him the busy activities of the day. After months of illness that had left her bedridden, Brenda had experienced two weeks of some improved health, and her stamina seemed to be returning. She was leaving to take her three-year-old granddaughter to her first ballet class. Her husband had plans to meet with some pastors in a neighboring town. Leaving the house, Brenda called out in the direction of her husband, "Love you Babe. See you later."

Brenda's husband decided to maximize a beautiful summer day. It would be perfect to take his motorcycle to the pastors' event. Not far from their home, as he headed out of town, a car that was coming from the other direction suddenly decided to turn onto the frontage road. They didn't see the motorcycle in the other lane and turned right into him. It was a direct hit with life and wreckage strewn across the road. A young college girl's life was changed forever and a beloved man's life taken. Without warning, Brenda's high school sweetheart was ripped from her loving arms. And just as suddenly, Brenda felt empty.

Only Hope Himself can help you walk through the valley of the shadow of death with no fear. Hope stands with you at the gravesite where shattered dreams and precious lives are buried together. Hope gives words of comfort to the bereaved so that they, in turn, can give them to others in need.

The funeral visitation of Brenda's husband filled with a long and growing line of mourners who came to pay their respects. In addition, nearly four miles of fellow motorcyclists came to pay tribute. Uniformed police officers, church members, community people and many others stood waiting in line for hours to give their condolences to the new widow.

To Brenda, it seemed like only yesterday that she had been standing next to another open casket, feeling empty and broken.

Nine years earlier their beautiful twenty-four-year-old daughter thought she had the flu. Without warning, her illness rapidly escalated into a rare blood virus, killing her within five days. Brenda now stood at her husband's casket with only her first-born daughter, her son-in-law and her grandchildren beside her.

Hope and Grace stood as invisible sentinels that day, enabling Brenda to comfort those who came to comfort her. Near the time of the funeral, which was to follow the visitation, the lines had to be closed in order to give the family a brief rest. One last mourner, a young girl, was left to talk to Brenda. Crying, the young girl told Brenda how very sorry she was over the death of Brenda's husband. Over the past three hours it seemed everyone had spoken similar words, yet Brenda never wearied of this repetitive comfort.

When Brenda's daughter locked eyes with the young mourner, she instantly recognized her as one of her former pre-school students from years ago. In a soul-to-soul exchange they looked deeply into one another's sorrowful eyes. Between deep sobs, the young girl identified herself as the one who had caused the deadly accident. That's when hope stepped in to lead the way, for only hope and grace can enable one to do what came next. Brenda, her daughter, and the nineteen-year-old walked to an empty side room to talk privately. Brenda now engaged the girl's eyes, with tears rushing down all of their cheeks. Brenda spoke life back into the troubled young lady with these three simple words: "I forgive you." She continued, "It was an *accident.*"

Hope opened a door to usher in a startling sense of freedom; the freedom to forgive and to be forgiven. Brenda and her daughter embraced the teen as they all wept together.

Brenda's enduring faith, and those of the stories before her—based on the historic empty tomb—continues to give her hope that one day she will see her husband. Hope reminds her of the promise, "I am the resurrection and the life. He who believes in me, though he may die, he shall live" (John 11:25).

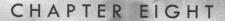

CHAPTER EIGHT

SURVIVORS

Hope can heal yesterday.

I am captivated by personal accounts from Holocaust survivors of World War II. Though a multitude of books have been published on this heart-wrenching subject and scores of movies have documented these atrocities, nothing is as powerful as hearing firsthand reports from Holocaust survivors.

Adolf Hitler was a demonically inspired madman who was obsessed with "ethnic cleansing." In Hitler's twisted vision of an ideal society he plotted the systematic end of his political enemies that included the elimination of *anyone* who didn't fit into the ideal "Aryan" race. He called for, and was largely successful in eliminating the physically handicapped, the mentally infirmed, the weak and the elderly, and those referred to as "sexual deviants." But above all the varied groups he thought to be inferior, Hitler fixated on the extinction of the Jewish race.

There were many veterans of this horrific war, along with prisoners who survived Hitler's concentration camps. Hope seemed to be AWOL. It was during this time that six million Jews were slaughtered, and those still in hiding wondered if they were next. It is imperative that their stories never die.

Back in 1942, Garmaine was just sixteen years old when she and her family were taken on a horrible trip. Told that they were going to be relocated to Poland and given homes and property, they were instead packed into cattle cars like a herd of livestock headed to slaughter. Garmaine and her family were clueless as to what awaited them in the cold-blooded prisons hidden in obscure places.

During their brutal, eight-day train ride, Garmaine, her mother, and her four sisters had no food or water. Their final destination was in fact Poland. Their new home would be the infamous concentration camp known as Auschwitz. Once unloaded, Garmaine was forcefully separated from her family. She was sent to Block 10 where three hundred young girls between the ages of twelve and twenty-eight endured shock treatments and sterilization. For reasons Garmaine would never know, her mother and sisters faced an even harsher sentence—they were sent to the gas chambers to die.

The Nazis believed the Jews were sub-human and referred to them as vermin. Consequently, Nazi surgeons refused to administer anesthesia to Jews going under the knife. In the midst of these inhumane conditions, Garmaine's brutal procedure was begun. After excising one of Garmaine's ovaries, the butcher's job was interrupted by a bombing raid. Before running for cover, the crazed Nazi surgeon pointed to his involuntary assistant, an imprisoned Jewish physician, and sternly commanded him to finish the job. Once he was assured they were alone, the Jewish surgeon leaned over Garmaine and whispered in her ear, "I must make an incision but I will *not* take your ovary." Next, the kind man warned Garmaine, "You must hide your monthly cycles." If his betrayal was ever exposed, both of their lives would be further endangered. Finally, this gentle doctor's last request offered Garmaine some tangible hope. "Remember me when you have children."

At the end of the war, Garmaine was freed and later married another Holocaust survivor. Together, they had four sons. She kept her word and named her first son after the Jewish doctor. Her first son—Sol Pitchon—is my friend.

Hope is visionary and sees beyond today. No one looked like they would ever be free from Hitler's evil resolve to kill all the Jews and eliminate whole classes of people. Sol has dedicated his life to helping women who are facing the crisis of an unplanned pregnancy. He devotes his life to exposing what he calls America's modern holocaust: abortion on demand. He works tirelessly in the Tampa Bay Area, where one-third of all pregnancies end in intentional termination. Since January 23, 1973, nearly sixty million defenseless unborn babies have perished, most of them needlessly. The fact that his own mother was mercifully allowed to have children makes Sol keenly sensitive to the silent cries of America's unborn. He remains passionate to help in life-affirming ways. Sol firmly believes the greatest travesty of justice is to willfully deprive others of life.

In the United States, the fight for life is more than a movement or cause. For our unborn citizens, it is a daily struggle. In a culture obsessed with selfish convenience, there is a growing temptation to devalue the lives of others. Your personal estimation of the value of the unborn may be skewed, if not challenged, by a trusted friend, mentor, or counselor.

I have a dear friend whose daughter and grandchild were legally killed by an abortion gone awry. A secret pregnancy was successfully terminated, but the shocking consequence was her daughter died in the procedure. She was overmedicated and lay dead with no emergency equipment on site and only the non-medical office receptionist to stand guard at her bedside. The doctor left her for forty-five minutes before any emergency services were called in order to terminate another pregnancy in the adjoining room.

I'll call my friend Jane Doe. Jane's immediate response was to focus on the killer's pending trial at the expense of tending to her own wrenching grief. Jane longed for his conviction. She passionately and tirelessly unearthed information in which the lawyer could find the necessary evidence to bring forth a guilty verdict. During a long three-year period, she took part in depositions and attended hearings.

On the third year anniversary of her daughter's death the doctor took a plea bargain and plead guilty. No trial ever took place. His prison sentence was woefully short, offensively light, and characterized by luxury. The doctor was sentenced to six months but only served three in a jail bed and breakfast that looked like a New England house with a white picket fence. Then he was given nine months' house arrest where he stayed in his own multi-million-dollar home on a peninsula surrounded by the ocean on three sides. He was a very wealthy Harvard Fellow who enjoyed the cover-ups inherent to his politically correct profession and his insider status.

This grave injustice plunged my emotionally exhausted friend into a dark pit of despair. Jane had not yet begun to grieve over these needless deaths beforehand and the demoralization of such a violent crime left her with no hope or reason to live. I once stayed on the phone with Jane through the night, helping her process her grief and anguish. Throughout her lengthy depression she was forthright about the suicidal state of her mind. She told her husband to take every gun out of the house. Jane's own life was in jeopardy. Her future felt hopeless. Jane confessed to me, "Every time I thought of suicide, I felt relief, almost joy. When I thought of continuing to live, I felt unbearable pain. It seemed a wonderful solution to my dilemma."

Thankfully, Jane's outlook changed and her reason to live strengthened when she became an advocate for life. Her passion now is to help others who are without hope and in crisis. Her daughter's story has been used to save other lives through billboard campaigns, radio and television interviews, and changing pertinent laws.

Clinical depression is no laughing matter. A brilliant comedian, loved by everyone, recently took his life, shocking the entire world. Since his passing, reports have shown how the deeply depressed sometimes mask their pain by bringing joy and laughter to others. No one could believe his depth of despair and hopelessness.

Suicide rates are alarming. It is reported to be the tenth leading cause of death in the United States. I admit, I do not understand mental illness, but I am glad for the continued outcry to better educate people about this life-threatening condition. My heart breaks for all who are impacted by a troubled mind. As I take a personal inventory of those I know lost to suicide, I am shocked. I must ask myself, like all those who have lost loved ones to this cruel fate, "What did I miss?"

Clinical depression is caused by a variety of factors, including the side effects of certain medications. Discouragement, grief and loss often contribute to a downward spiral, leaving the mind to contrive harmful solutions that can be fatal. Bi-polar symptoms are more than a moody personality. Chemical imbalances are dangerous unless properly diagnosed and treated. Common chemical imbalances might be easily remedied with dietary changes, while Seasonal Affective Disorder (SAD) is a cyclic depression linked to the limited amount of winter sunlight. To ignore depression and downplay the toll it takes on humanity is to ignore our Creator who designed mankind in three parts: body, mind, and spirit. This entire trio needs attention and support if we are to live balanced lives full of hope.

I am convinced the epitome of hopelessness is the act of choosing death over life. Every parent hopes their child will excel and be happy. No one imagines his or her own precious child secretly misfocused on suicide. The loss of any child for *any* reason is a great pain beyond words, but to lose a child to suicide is to know the depths of sorrow. Most parents want to protect their children, yet too many are left with feelings of helplessness as they grieve the loss of their child. Life's mission was aborted and over too soon.

Pastor Rick Warren impacts lives around the world as the author of the classic best seller, *The Purpose Driven Life*. One of Rick's abiding questions is, "What on earth are we here for?" His question has resonated with millions. Rick successfully contends that no one is an accident. Tragically, in the midst of his international outreach, Rick and his wife, Kay, faced the heartbreak of their own son's suicide. The world grieved with this famous family when the news spread quickly of their loss.

I recently listened to the message Pastor Warren shared sixteen weeks into his mourning process. The ripple effect of their tragedy gave me insight to the devastation that results when hope is blinded. Due to their heartache, Rick and his wife now extend a lifeline of hope to others who are facing similar temptations to take their life. One passage Rick shared that helped him focus through the pain was his repeated reminder to "Stand firm in hope."

Tony Dungy, a former coach of NFL's Indianapolis Colts, speaks openly about his son's suicide in a sincere attempt to help others through their similar crises. He repurposes his personal pain to help others find salvation and peace of mind as he assures them of hope beyond this life.

Self-loathing and hatred are two other avenues to hopelessness. Hatred, like that exhibited in gang violence and deliberately spread by racial injustice, tries to assassinate hope. Fear and isolation resist hope. Where do we deposit the horrors of yesterday in order to live for today? Hope can heal yesterday.

Post-Traumatic Stress Disorder (PTSD), another sinister enemy of hope, has long plagued victims of violent crimes and domestic violence or ritualistic abuse. It has now come to the forefront of America's conscience as tens of thousands of our returning soldiers are haunted by PTSD and other manifestations of survivor's guilt. At this writing, twenty-two veterans commit suicide daily. Too often, these loyal defenders of freedom are prisoners of a silent, psychological warfare long after their active duty has ended. Vivid memories of the brutalities of combat resurface as night terrors and imprison many in dark depression.

Coming home to our nation without any accolades or words of gratitude is cruel and unpatriotic. Yet, such was the everyday reality of our returning Korean and Vietnam veterans. Thankfully, we have learned a lesson at their expense. Today, the new norm is to support our troops in the field of combat (regardless of our political views) and provide tangible support to military families while their soldier is deployed. In a show of deepest gratitude, we acknowledge their ongoing sacrifice that protects our costly freedoms. The noble act of laying down their lives should not be confused with a reason to take their own lives. Hope brought them home and hope can reset their future.

At all costs, life is to be protected. Life is filled with potential by divine design. All that you and I have experienced has merit. No matter the prison you are in presently, ask for help. Help brings hope into the picture, and hope is the great liberator.

CHAPTER NINE

CROWNS

*Hope stays the course even when
your path is blurred by the storms.*

The other day I researched some of the top things that create stress. Among some on the list were: loss of a job, moving, divorce, death of a loved one, and illness. However, one other at the top of the list should have been seeing the dentist. If you are able to be at peace through the actual procedure, with your mouth stuffed to the gills with foreign objects and the sound of drills, then wait for the bill to send you to a new level of stress.

I am blessed to have a fantastic dentist. Dr. Glenn is a friend who is kind and tells you everything he is about to do. The struggle for me, beyond elevated blood pressure, is my wanting to talk to him when he is in the middle of placing something else in my mouth. We love his family and our sons have played baseball together for years. Is it my imagination, or does he ask questions right before another tool is placed in my mouth? It is embarrassing to gag on the large X-ray cardboard contraption, and drool all over the front of the paper bib. The chiseling sound of plaque removal and the dreaded questions about flossing are hard too. Water sprayed around your fillings to see if there is a new crack can send you nearly out of the chair when the discovery is made. The verdict over what needs to be done next can take your breath away. Once when my blood pressure had returned nearly to normal, I found a quick moment to tell Dr. Glenn a verse of scripture I suggested for his marketing strategy.

"Hey Doc! This verse is yours. 'Open your mouth wide and I will fill it,' says the Lord." We both laughed—and then the drill started all over. Anticipating some unfavorable changes in my molars, Dr. Glenn said, "Gail, I see crowns in your future." I love the idea of royalty. And perhaps for some that is the ultimate dream, but these crowns are different. He continued, "In fact, Gail, you need seven crowns." There was no getting out of this costly predicament. Having a full set of teeth seemed appealing since I am a public speaker. There was nothing to do but overcome the stress and pray I strike gold soon.

The phrase, "I see crowns in your future" has never left me, even after the completion of all the dental work. Since America broke away from England over two centuries ago, our democracy replaced the monarchy and crowns were old school. Our only reminder that crowns still exist is to watch the royal heirs and their future from across the pond. But, for the rest of us, life seems rather average. Is it really though? What if we knew we had a high calling, with royal assignments and representing something bigger than ourselves? Would it give us more hope for living?

I am intrigued with crowns. In Major League Baseball there is a Triple Crown that celebrates the player who has the most runs batted in (RBI), home runs, and the highest batting average in a given season. It is a difficult and rare achievement. Miguel Cabrera in 2012 and Carl Yastrzemski in 1967 were the last to win this prestigious award.

Another Triple Crown captured the world's attention by one of the most popular horses, "American Pharoah." In case you think it a typo, the spelling of his name is correct, though wrong according to the proper spelling. Even his Triple Crown winning blanket has his named spelled the right way—but wrong according to his registration. In a mistake, the name was registered with the Jockey Club in both spellings to assure that no other horse would ever have his winning name. He was named through a contest on social media. No doubt, there has never been another like this brilliant champion whose temperament is gentle and his long strides smooth and fast.

In 2015 this thoroughbred racehorse won the American Triple Crown and the Breeders' Cup Classic. By doing so, he became the first horse to win the "Grand Slam" of American horse racing. He was bred and owned throughout his racing career by Ahmed Zagat of Zagat Stables and trained by Bob Baffert.

He ran poorly in his track debut as a two-year-old but won his next races by several lengths. An injury kept him out of the Breeders' Cup Juvenile, but the impression left from his previous wins resulted in his being named the American Champion Two-Year-Old Horse at the 2014 Eclipse Awards.

He began his 2015 campaign with wins at the Rebel Stakes and the Arkansas Derby. He went on to win the Kentucky Derby, the Preakness Stakes, and the Belmont Stakes, becoming the first American Triple Crown winner since Affirmed in 1978 and the twelfth in history. He posted the second-fastest winning time for a Triple Crown winner with a closing quarter-mile time, faster than that of Secretariat in 1973.

He then left Monmouth Park and Haskell Invitational behind him with two more wins. His eight-race winning streak at Traver's Stakes was snapped when he finished a close second. After a two-month layoff he won the Breeders' Cup Classic, challenging older horses for the first time and winning by six-and-a-half lengths, and breaking a track record.

American Pharoah even won races under adverse conditions by running in rain and mud, easily dominating the field. A professional basketball coach suggested American Pharoah was the only athlete better than LeBron James. He was pictured in *Vogue* and *Sports Illustrated* and appeared on the *Today Show*, where he stood calmly between his trainer and rider who were settled into director's chairs.

Born on Groundhog's day, with a faint star on his forehead, the only white on his body, American Pharoah is beautiful. His tail is shortened due to an unconfirmed report that he was chased by a mountain lion and his tail was as close as the lion could get because of champion speed.

His talent, skill and personality have won hearts around the globe. Though initially irritated by crowds, his teachable spirit submitted to his trainer's placing cotton in his ears, after which he eventually began to reflect a gentle demeanor. At the completion of his final race that made him the Triple Crown Champion he was led into the middle of thirty reporters who were allowed to pet and even kiss him. The *New York Times* described American Pharoah's Keeneland win as "sealing his legacy as a horse for the ages."

Now that you are mindful of a champion, let's unpack this horse-sense for any wavering you might have in your hopes to excel. You, too, have crowns in your future—if you want them. American Pharoah's story is similar to yours. His name, like yours, no matter how it is spelled, never stopped the gift that was in him. However, it may still take some training and a teachable spirit. What do you have to lose as you spend the time and pay the price to achieve the next difficult race? Most are spending their energies on a treadmill in life going nowhere. There is more.

Just like American Pharoah was given remedies for his jitters and agitation, you may need to do the same to get hope to a peak level. The cotton in his ears helped keep out the constant noise that stole his focus and energy. Your own head noise, old recordings of failure and negative talk, keeps you running in circles and returning to the same place, time and time again. Old voices of fear and doubt and critics on the sidelines prevent your advancement. It is time to hear the encouragement from those who are cheering you on to greater challenges and the successes to follow.

I have a friend from Zimbabwe who tells others to place their hand on their heads and pray, "Expand my capacity." Any ability can be expanded, not to mention your own dreams. Also, American Pharoah wanted to see the bigger view. Blinders may work for some who cannot focus, but in time, you must see more than a narrow space. To expand is doable. Do not lose hope if you cannot see the bigger possibility. It is still there.

I love that a champion could perform, yet be great with people. I believe this is essential in leadership. Does your demeanor allow people to approach you? American Pharoah trained to have these skills. Whether through coaching, training, or mentoring, get what is needed to win at every level. The task may be remembered, but it is the legacy that is left, through people, that your efforts and work will carry on. The hope for each of us should be to have vision for the generation who follows our lead. Give them something of value to duplicate. Breed other's dreams and ideas with your seasoned counsel and encouragement.

We hope for perfect conditions—but that is not reality. Just like American Pharoah, the races that prepared him the most were the ones with the challenges of bad weather and an undesirable track. Perhaps your own storms have prepared you more than you know. What you have already lived through has made you ready for the future. What if, like the champion racehorse, it is something that will give you an advantage? You, too, can conquer the elements and captivate your field. Hope cheers from the stands, "Keep running!" Hope stays the course even in those times when your path is blurred by the storms. There is a race to finish and a prize to be won.

Champions never quit. Finish well. Hope rides with you.

CHAPTER TEN

LICENSE

Hope allows you to hold out for a
possible solution.

My driver's license was the last thing I gave up when my eyesight worsened. No doubt, it should have been the first thing to go, but the surrender of such a prized possession was intricately attached to my independence.

In those years, we lived in Illinois where the roads were straight lines in flat terrain and where, it seemed, anyone could drive blindfolded. Believe me when I say, I tried. When you need to ask your front seat passenger to tell you where the road is and where the stop sign is located, the jig is up.

Moving to Dallas in 2000 excited me when I realized I finally lived in a city where even a blind woman could most likely get a license. All the drivers seemed like they were blind too. The traffic and driving in Dallas is crazy. Unfortunately, the best legal compromise for me was my Texas photo I.D. Occasionally I have driven on back country roads, or through pastures, with the help of the brave passenger who let me enjoy the fun. But, for the most part, I have learned to be content with a chauffeur—for the time being.

Just like a driver's license, a photo I.D. must be updated periodically. My busy schedule had kept me from doing this in a timely manner. To tell you the truth, I had forgotten about it. We were booked to fly to a speaking engagement in a few days and my not having a current I.D. would be non-negotiable for the TSA agents.

I love to make a memory so I had an elaborate plan for our excursion to the Department of Public Safety (DPS). One morning I suggested to Tony that we drive north of Dallas to a small town to get my new I.D. I didn't want to mess with the long lines of the city. Plus, we could catch lunch along the way. It would be fun. Tony agreed and we took off. He was more focused on the task at hand, while I was all about making new memories along the journey. Our targeted town was so small that we nearly missed the DPS office as it sat, unassumingly, alongside the highway.

Only five people were in line when we entered the building. The first sign Tony read clearly stated that cash was the only acceptable method of payment.

Tony sighed and said, "I need to find the nearest ATM. Will you be okay by yourself?"

Though not ideal to be left alone, and wondering if he would get back in time, I drew a deep breath, as I sized up my new surroundings. "Sure, go on. I will find my way. But, try to hurry."

No sooner had Tony left than my adventure started. I decided the room was way too quiet. So, my first order of business was to liven up the place! I have never met a stranger in life and truly believe that all are worth knowing. Plus, I anticipated needing someone to tell me when the line moved. I quickly started a conversation with those closest to me in line. I use casual conversation to look for common ground on which to build new relationships.

One gentleman lived near where we once did. Another gal was new to the state but came from an area where I had visited several times. The woman behind me was a nurse and cancer survivor. We talked about the upcoming walk to raise funds for cancer research.

The time flew as my world was enriched. Soon I was engaged with several people as the line continued to advance. Then it was my turn to go to the counter. Thankfully, I heard my husband's winded voice as he excused himself while moving to the front of the line.

I stepped up to the counter and cheerfully said, "Good morning."

The DPS agent was anything but friendly. In fact, she was terribly grumpy. I decided to cheerfully state my needs. "Ma'am, I am here to update my photo I.D." The gruff agent barely acknowledged I had spoken to her. Just the same, I continued. "Ma'am. My name is Gail McWilliams. I lost my eyesight so if there are any papers to fill out, my husband is here to help me."

She managed a faint, "Okay." While I stood thinking things over, I decided to confess what had become obvious to me.

"Ma'am. I want to apologize. I think my I.D. expired some time ago."

Without missing a beat, the DPS agent leaned in towards me and said, "How would you even know?"

Without thinking, I automatically leaned in towards her and said, "Well. The other day when the cops pulled me over…" My unexpected wit completely disarmed her and she laughed big. So did the rest of the formerly quiet room of on-lookers.

In that instant, the atmosphere changed and I won a friend. The agent smiled and said, "Lady. You've made my day!"

Defusing anger is a social skill everyone needs to learn. It takes the same amount of time to thoughtfully respond as it takes to mindlessly react to the hostile situations we sometimes face.

It is easy to be offended. A stranger's super-sensitivity is not really about you or your personality but about their lack of preparation for the real world. Lack of manners, rudeness and inability to be kind to others often stems from parental neglect and withheld training. This social deficit is tragically passed down through generations of families who were never taught either.

Then, too, there are those who were instructed well as children but never grew up. They live self-absorbed lives. Talk about blindness! I say, win a heart as you take the higher road. Conversation that is constantly weighed down with petty offenses reflects an unhappy life, like the lingering stench of a landfill on a hot, humid day. Have you ever stopped to consider that your unrealistic expectations of others are actually pre-meditated grudges? In a nutshell, quit looking for a fight.

Be quick to forgive.

Overlook the error of those who blindly bump into your sore spots. Time is needlessly wasted in conversation by people who simultaneously take offensive and defensive postures. How on earth do they hope to reach their goals unscathed when they are busy with all the pushbacks in this game called life? Run on and shake off the potential setbacks. Life is about more than one small game. It is a championship play-off.

During preparation for a very important bowl game one of the competing team's quarterbacks chose to be part of a fight in a bar after curfew. His angry reaction caused a domino effect of consequences that impacted not just him, but the whole team. The quarterback's performance had been recognized that season as outstanding; however, he was disqualified for the last game of the season, leaving people angry and puzzled. Their chances for a win were put in jeopardy.

Be sobered to know your actions and reactions will inadvertently affect more than just you. An offense to which you angrily react is a trap. If you hope to have success in life it will take a wisely executed game plan.

I asked a successful attorney the secret for his years of winning cases. He told me that he first approaches the opposing side in humility. His first question is "How can we resolve this situation so it is beneficial for both sides?" His specialty is litigation, but his goal is to work for an equitable settlement. His cases are masterfully prepared. Even judges compliment him on his skill and extensive preparation. The victory starts long before any trial. He gains ground by a humble lead instead of the stereotypical arrogance expected by one with his track record. Wouldn't the same approach work with breeches in relationships?

The art of winning hearts is like a game to me. I face the same challenges and obstacles that everyone encounters when working closely with the public. Some days I am better at my game than others. There are still times when I react. I can't help but wonder what is wrong with people. But for the most part, I try to engage with mankind and become an unforgettable part of their day. I am determined that the atmosphere of my day will be set by my tone and my vision, not by another's mood or reaction.

Hope sees beyond it all.

If you think I have mastered living with no reaction, then let me be the first to take myself off the short pedestal. My default mode is defense. Unfortunately, I am tempted to be the most defensive with my family and those that mean the most to me. This is often due to my not listening carefully or not taking time to understand. It's impossible to accurately hear what someone is saying if, when they speak, you are already building your case in your mind and drafting up your defense statement. The art of listening attentively will reveal multiple layers of meaning. Perhaps the real hindrance in communicating effectively comes by way of wanting to do things speedily with minimal effort.

Our great-grandmothers had a saying for this: simply, "Haste makes waste." In the long run, that which we do hastily usually ends up taking more time to repair. Rebuilding broken pieces shattered by reckless actions is more difficult than new construction.

What's the bottom line when it comes to dealing with difficult people? My constructive observation is to remind you that hope is patient and always sees the best. Hope allows you to hold out for a possible solution. I believe the difference between reacting and responding is a person's focus. If everything is about you and how you feel, it is impossible to get through a day emotionally unharmed. In our touchy-feely culture, offenses abound and misunderstandings are the norm. When you focus on others and their needs with the sincere intention of making a difference in your generation, each activity, outing, interaction and event reveals hidden treasure.

One special, personal bonus for me is I get great "material" along the way. So, brush that chip off your shoulder, or *you* might become an object lesson in my next book!

Let hope help you see the big picture and live free of resentment and anger.

CHAPTER ELEVEN

ANTS

*Hope keeps it's footing in our lives
by its ability to seek out a bigger
purpose.*

An entire book could be published on my parents' amazing life together, the friends they have made and the lives they have touched during the course of their marriage of sixty-plus years. They have been happily married except for the one fight they had which Dad shares openly with all who are interested. When asked how on earth they could have had only *one* spat, he promptly replies, "Oh, it started sixty years ago." Laughing, he explains that its outcome is still up for grabs. My parents raised a wonderful family, enjoyed a successful career, and they continue to be active in church as they make friends across the world. Nothing has changed in their sunset years, except their pace.

Mom and Dad have certainly endured setbacks and times of severe testing. Yet, they remain full of hope, trusting their future to God's care. In her seventies, Mom was car-jacked and left for dead, with her back broken in two places. A few years later, Dad underwent emergency open-heart surgery when tests proved his heart was only operating at 17% of its capacity. Mom waited in hopeful expectation that God would spare his life. Through it all, my parents continue to love people and serve others. They understand what life is about and, no matter the challenge, their unstoppable faith and love never waver.

When it comes to my Dad's comedic acts, Mom is his best audience. With his Southeast Missouri humor, wit and timing, Dad easily makes Mom laugh every day. Dad claims that Mom is gullible. Therefore, he has always played his best pranks on her. Mom also scares easily, so Dad takes advantage of this with his soft-footed walk. I love to hear him laugh when he tells us how he "caught Mom" again with another of his practical jokes. This prank is my personal favorite.

Mom loves order and neatness, so insects of any kind are intolerable. Unfortunately, Mom saw a couple of ants in their master bathroom one afternoon. Dad claims she had poison and sticky paper in every nook and cranny in hopes of catching the two lone intruders. While Mom was in the other end of the house, Dad went to the kitchen and grabbed the pepper and sprinkled it generously in one of the bathroom sinks, then quietly returned to his office to work at his computer. He'd barely sat down when he heard Mom yell his name in horror and told him to come fast. Dad walked briskly to rescue his bride. With his background in engineering and as a leader in his field, Dad can fix problems of any size.

"Look at the ants in the sink!" she exclaimed in horror. "The whole *colony* has moved in!"

Dad leaned over the sink with Mom to examine the multiplying little pests. Dad acted concerned as he joined in. Time passed in silence. Mom studiously observed that the ants were not moving. In fact, they were not even the same size as the two original invaders. With their heads still close together, Mom and Dad stared down at the sink. Then, Mom slowly turned to look at Dad. When their eyes met, she shook her head and said, "You did it to me again!" She laughed loudly as Dad quietly smiled. Mom had fallen into Dad's clever trap while her two ants ran for cover. Mom may be gullible but she's a good sport.

Hope keeps it's footing in our lives by its ability to seek out a bigger purpose. Just like the ants that Mom feared were multiplying in her sink, our first impressions are often flawed. Our perception will benefit from a closer examination of the facts. Fears are egotistical: they puff themselves up to exaggerate their importance. Fear wrestles against hope, determined to knock out joy and leave you hopeless. Nonsense. Two ants do not a sink-full make.

I love to tell this simple ant story to shine a light on the power of fear. If not examined closely, fear can extinguish any flicker of hope. When hope wavers, mental imposters rush into our lives in the form of worries that continually forecast fears that may or may not have merit. Fear is an exhausting, unwelcome guest in our busy minds, so why do we keep inviting it for return visits? That which we fear the most rarely happens. Meanwhile, our physical and emotional health is at risk.

Worry is placing faith in what might happen. Hope simply says, but what if it *doesn't* happen? Worry is a chronic addiction for some and only takes away from this present moment. Life is filled with moments too precious to share with the negativity of worry, fear, and anxiety. Resolve to rest in hope. Just like the ants, deal with what is real and wash the rest of your worries down the drain. Some fears *appear* to be real, but look closer. Is hope in your midst? Hope usually offers a strategy for navigating through your present ordeal. Fear is always an enemy of hope. It is futile for us to attempt to deal with things out of our control. Sometimes waiting in hope is the only sane posture to take.

In the midst of life-threatening circumstances, you can still enjoy life's unpredictable journey. You might be surprised to learn that during my Dad's ant-tics, his health had been failing and his heart was severely weakened. But his mind was intact and his effort to live life with joy and purpose countered any worry or preoccupation with self. Following Dad's open-heart surgery (and his near death experience) the exhausting struggle and battle for recovery ensued. Mom was hyper-vigilant in caring for her dearest friend.

One day, while supposedly napping, Dad heard Mom softly open the door to check on her patient as he slept. As she tiptoed across the room, Dad decided to play a trick on her by holding his breath. Mom looked at him and was frightened that he was not breathing. As she leaned in closer to listen to him, Dad opened his smiling eyes and looked up at her, asking, "Did you think I was dead?"

This was one time she didn't find any humor in one of his tricks. Dad likes to tell the story, though, and still thinks it's funny. You see, in the midst of her prolonged worry and physical strain, Mom was beginning to lose her joy.

What does joy need to sustain itself? Joy relies on hope. When circumstances are beyond your control, joy becomes a deliberate choice. Eternity is settled for my parents because of another choice they each made earlier in life. Therefore, they see each day as a gift. Keeping tabs on your day-to-day joy levels is a proactive approach to safeguarding hope. Both feed off one another.

Have you ever considered the reality of what you fear? Therapists often coach their clients to challenge their own thought process by asking themselves, "What is the worst thing that could happen?" Have you ever tried this? It really works! This simple mental exercise empowers you to think through the fear that threatens to consume you. Think of it as drawing a line in the sand of your overactive imagination and declaring, "*This* is where I draw the line!" Courageously facing the unreasonable nature of your worst fears sets you free to mentally construct a plan of action.

Hope is the perfect antidote for fear. True hope trusts confidently. The promise that "all things work together for good" is yours for the taking. Examine what you fear and why. The fear of failure is easily offset by the hope of learning from your mistakes so you won't waste time repeating them. Failure triumphantly announces to your soul, *You're getting closer!* Then, hope shouts back, *Try again!*

The fear of what others think of us *when* we fail shows how narcissistic we truly are. We wrongly imagine that everyone watches our every move. Each new day fresh opportunity comes, wrapped in hope, so stop worrying about what others think about you.

Take a long look at the toll fear has taken in your life. Aren't you weary of the fearful thoughts that occupy your mind? Do you see how they siphon off energy and divert your focus? Then, what are you waiting for? Get busy sorting the pepper from the ants! Exchange the torment of fear with joyful hope and remind yourself that *nothing* is unconquerable.

Choose to live with hope that sees beyond your present predicament. This, too, shall pass.

CHAPTER TWELVE

DINA

Hope makes history.

I love a great sports story, especially one where the hero of the story has the character to match their gift. Players who come out of obscurity to make it big inspire me. My vote for MVP is tied between the underdog who overcomes adversity and the proverbial comeback kid. In either case, the most exciting games are the ones won by a single goal played by a lone player in the final seconds of the game.

One of my favorite champions was showcased in the 1990 NCAA Division III women's championship basketball game. Talk about winning against all hope. And, to make the story even better, the winning team was from Hope College. In fact, that night Hope made history! Let me set the stage.

Dina Disney was born and raised in Kentucky, the second daughter of a basketball enthusiast. She was the tomboy who shadowed her dad to all his basketball leagues and recreational teams, learning the game by studying her father's every move on the court. At the tender age of five Dina picked up her first basketball. She religiously practiced the fundamentals throughout her elementary and junior high school years, and by the time Dina entered high school, she daily shot two hundred free throws. By all accounts it seemed nothing would keep Dina from her dream of becoming a basketball champion. During high school Dina helped her team advance to Kentucky's state-level tournament. She set a new record as the highest scorer, 1,486 points. This record wasn't eclipsed for another twenty-eight years.

Her efforts paid off by way of scholarship offers to several colleges. She chose Georgetown University, in Georgetown, Kentucky, because she wanted to be near her Kentucky home and family. Unfortunately, Dina blew out her knee just before the season began during her first year of college. After three weeks of rehab she was back on the court. She learned to endure whatever it took to play the game. Then, an additional injury in the middle of a jumping layup caused Dina to crawl off the court. Surgery was needed to repair the torn ligament in her knee. But, unlike today's minimally invasive procedure, Dina's rehab was prolonged and her recovery was tedious. The torn ligaments were stitched tightly back into place, resulting in limited flexibility.

Dina was red-shirted her freshman year of college ball so her knee could thoroughly heal. She is often asked if it was hard to sit on the bench when she was accustomed to the starting lineup. She answers, "No, I learned more about the game watching from the bench."

Dina gained a new awareness that every team has great talent sitting on the bench, waiting for the opportunity to play. Dina believes that enduring those trials ultimately made her a better coach later in her life.

Following the necessary surgery to repair her knee, the surgeon privately informed her parents of the grim reality. He emphatically prophesied, "Dina will never play again." Her parents wisely kept the surgeon's prognosis to themselves.

Between her sophomore and junior year, new doors of opportunity opened for Dina. She played basketball in Ecuador with Athletes in Action. She loved her time there and connected well with her coach on the trip, who happened to coach the girls' varsity team at Hope College, a school she was unfamiliar with, in Holland, Michigan. Dina was looking for a change and decided to move away from her Kentucky home for her remaining two years of collegiate study.

She transferred to Hope College in the fall of 1988. Sadly, after a year, the team's favorite coach was released from her position. It was difficult for the entire team to press on under the emotional stress of losing their coach, but they were determined to have a winning season in her honor. Their strategy worked. The team qualified for the NCAA tournament. They just kept winning. Dina Disney called them a "Cinderella team." They were relative unknowns.

In March, Holland, Michigan, was chosen to host the 1990 NCAA Division III women's basketball championship, and Hope College was one of the surprise contenders. The final game was determined through highly competitive days of play, and Hope was the underdog, going into the championship game with little recognition. A team out of New York was the favored team to win.

Dina's new boyfriend, Jeff, brought flowers to the game that night but left them in the car. He planned to bring them inside the noisy arena during halftime to be ready to give them to her after the game. However, the score and forecast of the game made him decide to leave the flowers in the car—things did not look great for a win.

With eight minutes left the Hope team was down twenty points. Dina and her team made a plea with the coach that they press hard and change up their original game plans. Hope's coach consented, and press they did! The team progressively closed the gap, and the score was too close to call near the game's end.

With only twenty seconds to go, Dina shot a three-pointer from the corner and tied the score. The crowd went crazy with excitement and they were on their feet with explosive cheers. Hope had turned the game on its ear.

With only ten seconds on the clock, Dina remembered the scouting reports. The tall player she guarded liked to move left and Dina anticipated her every move. When Dina moved to block her, the point guard charged into her. A foul was called on the opposing player and the ball was put back into the possession of the Flying Dutch.

With only four seconds left Hope threw the ball to half court where a scramble took place. Dina found herself with the ball with only one thing left to do. She chucked the ball from half court, which fell woefully short. But, in the process she was fouled.

Then it was noticed by the referees that the clock indicated there was no time left. Two big zeros illuminated Hope's biggest concern. But, had the buzzer sounded or not? The loudness of the fans in that arena may have masked the buzzers sound. If it *had* gone off, then the foul may have occurred after it sounded, and the game would go into overtime. If the buzzer had not gone off, then the foul occurred before the buzzer and free throws by Dina would be in order. The referees moved for the timekeeper to simply start the clock. Upon doing so, the buzzer sounded, meaning there was, indeed, time left on the clock when the foul occurred.

They placed the clock back to as close to less than one second as possible and Dina headed to the free throw line. During the thunderous noise Dina looked up into the crowd to spot her mom, who was pointing heavenward. Dina looked down to her shoe on the weakened knee side where her laces were configured in the shape of a cross. As she positioned herself at the line, she coached herself, saying, "I can do all things through Christ who strengthens me."

Dina told me that a shooter has a good sense when they release the ball if it is going to make the basket before it actually does. Dina watched with the crowd as the ball spun towards its goal. The ecstatic crowd was held in suspense, and all were on their feet. Then, her hoop swished—not once, but *twice*—and these first-time NCAA Champions put Hope College on the map with a 65 to 63 win.

The court flooded with fans, along with Dina's family, friends and teammates. Dina and her mother found one another and embraced in tears. Only then did Dina's mother tell her, "The doctor said you would never play again. I didn't want you to know until now."

The biggest game in the history of Hope College athletics was played that night. It was the night when Hope made history.

I am not sure what your next move will be or the game plan of your life, but it is not too late. Practice the fundamentals of hope that see beyond the apparent time, and keep pressing on. Don't give in to defeat without a full-court press. Stay in the lane of hope, even when the odds are against you, even if you're not favored to win.

While writing this chapter, college football history was made in a bowl game between the Oregon Ducks and Texas Christian University. At halftime, TCU was not even on the scoreboard. In fact, Texas fans left the stadium by the droves, and fans at home turned off the game.

Evidently, the coach's motivational speech at halftime proved to be a game changer. In three overtimes, the TCU Horn Frogs came back to win the game 47 to 41, making it one of the biggest comebacks in NCAA history. Why don't *you* be the next comeback kid? There is yet time to get off the 50-yard line and move down the field of life!

Don't let the ticking of your internal clock distract you from the singular choice before you. Calm your nerves by rehearsing words that inspire you to reach for your goals. I love the lasting result of Dina's amazing championship win. She said, "That single victory has given me a passion for the impossible."

Time may be running out, but nothing is impossible. Never lose hope.

CHAPTER THIRTEEN

BOISE

Joy is a choice birthed in hope.

One weekend I was a featured speaker at a women's conference in Boise, Idaho. It was my first visit to this treasured gem, surrounded by mountains, known as the foothills of the Rockies. The mountain bluebird hovers over the beauty of some of the longest white water rivers, and there are hikers, bikers, elk hunters, and loads of people fishing. No wonder the director only offered me two possible dates for the autumn conference, because it had to be between deer and elk hunting season. When I inquired, "Is this a problem, since the ladies will need to be home to care for the children while the men hunt?" She immediately replied, "Oh no. Here, women are some of the best hunters." Later, I discovered that she was one of the top female elk hunters in the state. It is hard to imagine now, when I think back to when she picked us up at the airport, that her normal camouflaged hunting gear was replaced with tall stiletto heels and stylish colorful blazer.

In this vast Idaho outdoor arena, lined with miles of timber, discoveries are limitless. You can visit the largest French fry factory in the world, one of the many places in the state where the Idaho potato rules. And, more meaningful to me is the state motto: *esto perpetua*. It means, "It is forever." This is indeed the description of my priceless souvenir I received that joyful weekend.

Finally, the date was chosen and the stage set for a weekend of the tender and the tough, all gathered in the Civic Center for an unforgettable conference, entitled, "Contagious Joy." Excited, I was ready for my five presentations in two days.

While preparing for the conference, I discovered it is impossible to have joy without hope. One day I was reading the scriptures and stumbled over what seemed to be an oxymoron. I was in the book of James where he said to count it all joy when you fall into various trials. How could that be? Rereading the verse over and over I asked myself, "Why would you do that?" Dear old James was not trying to produce masochists. Instead, he was trying to redirect our focus. The joy isn't in the trial, but in the one who delivers you out of the trial. And, that, my friend, generates hope. Whatever you are facing is temporary, and hope not only helps you get through a trial but also, many times, gives you an alternate path or an exit ramp from the trial. When hope delivers there is joy in abundance. When you choose to focus on your trouble you reduce your capacity for joy and subsequently, for the hope you need to navigate your distress.

I am convinced that hope has a sense of humor. It sees beyond where you are today and joyfully anticipates your transition from trial to triumph. Hope helps you rejoice once you see that today's problem can be tomorrow's testimony.

Upon landing in Boise, my husband spotted the new Boise State University plane sitting near our gate. Its vibrant colors, with their mascot emblem on the tail, were impressive. That year BSU had captured the world's attention with their outstanding college football team's extraordinary performance. My dad helped me keep up with the team once he heard I was going to Boise. He knows I like to cheer for the underdog. I could feel joy mounting inside me as I anticipated what lay ahead.

Traveling often has some challenges, especially when you cannot see and your arms are filled with a large purse and carry-on luggage, not to mention our snack bag for the plane. However, Tony and I have created a dance that works well for us. We place a four-wheel roller suitcase between us, with the extended handle for us both to hold. His hand is first and mine follows his lead. We can move efficiently down any airport corridor. Along our way, I encountered an unexpected detour while headed to the baggage carousel.

I heard a sound that caught my attention. Without warning, I removed my hand from the luggage to stop dead in my tracks. "Where is that laughter coming from?" I asked aloud. Previously, on the flight, I used my travel hours to review my weekend of notes on the subject of joy. Now I was determined to see where this hysterical laughter was coming from in the Boise airport. Its sound grew louder, and I was about to join in. It was contagious.

Tony, on the other hand, was clueless that he had lost his traveling companion. He was on a mission to get our other luggage, obviously, with or without me. The laughter kept increasing while I stood in the middle of people passing me. By now, I started laughing out loud too. I had to know before going on. Where could all the gaiety be and why?

Standing alone, looking straight ahead, but listening intently, I now heard a familiar voice. "Why did you let go?" Tony asked, with some irritation. I told him of my quest and that I wasn't moving until I knew the source of this laughter. I am sure that at times like this his facial expressions must include sheer disbelief, some rolling of the eyes, and looks of frustration concerning the woman God gave him. However, I was not moved by anything except to solve the mystery of where all the joy was coming from.

Trying to talk through my giggles, I said, "Tony, would you please go find out who is laughing and why?" My husband, not finding any humor in the sound, hesitantly consented to my request and within moments came back with the answer. "Gail, there are little toy animals in a gift shop and each of them have different laughs."

"Oh, I must have one!" I said. "This will be a great visual for me to use in one of the sessions!"

Tony left to go make the purchase as I stood in the same spot in the corridor, still laughing aloud. A woman stopped to stand and listen with me, asking, "Where's all that laughter coming from?" I told her about the toy animals in one of the gift shops and how I had just sent my husband to go purchase one. Immediately we started to talk like we already knew each other.

"What brings you to Boise?" she asked. I replied, "I'm here to speak for a conference at the Boise Civic Center. "What about you?"

She enthusiastically said, "Me too, my husband and I are here to speak for a conference at the Nazarene College."

"I told her about the theme of my teaching sessions and how well my new laughing pet would showcase the concept of "contagious joy." She asked me how I would use my new discovery. I told her I was not sure but would find a way.

One question led to another, and before very long I told her my story about gradually losing my eyesight after having our children. I assured her that my eyesight may be impaired, but my vision was keen. She then told me *her* story about how she lost the sight of one of her eyes in a tragic accident. By this time, we were walking together, and I had no idea where I had left my husband nor did she know where hers had gone either. Somehow, in that moment, it didn't even matter. We quickly agreed that we would be new friends. We laughed, that between the two of us, we only had one good eye! Nevertheless, I could clearly see that I had just met a friend who would be in my life for years to come.

It is true that Carol and I remain friends to this day. Both of us have busy traveling schedules, yet we e-mail or call each other randomly and always just pick up where we left off. She identifies herself as My Boise Friend.

How could I forget such an encounter and my "forever" souvenir? In a world where our schedules are full and our lives are overbooked, we fail to stop along the way and listen. Too often, our plans are written in concrete, leaving little flexibility in which to enjoy life and the delightful surprises that come with it.

A simple conversation has the potential to become a lifetime friendship. A word of encouragement keeps you relevant in the game of inspiring others to reach for more. A word of kindness is a gift you can give to others, no matter their position. As you give yourself more freely to a day, your ordinary routine soon becomes extra-ordinary.

I am often asked, "How can you have so much joy when you cannot see?" I soundly reply, "How can you *see* and have no joy?" Joy is a choice birthed in hope. My passion fuels me, but my purpose drives me. No matter my physical state, there are treasures to unearth and new levels of joy-filled hope to experience.

The crazy end to my Boise story was the flight home. Instead of departing on Sunday afternoon, as is customary for most conference goers, Tony and I flew back to Dallas on Monday afternoon. And, guess what? My new friend was on the same flight! After takeoff, she exchanged seats with my husband, and we talked non-stop all the way to our connecting city. We laughed and talked like childhood friends.

Take time to notice what surrounds you. Learn to treasure the golden moments and those you find in it. Many treasures exist in the divine connections developing right in front of you.

Keep your eyes open and stand in joyful hope.

CHAPTER FOURTEEN

DUNES

*There is no road or path you travel
where hope does not reach to
steady you.*

E ven in the deserts of life, each new day is a gift filled with layered treasures. The memory of one such treasure still makes me laugh.

While I was touring and speaking in the Southwest, I had a day off. Our daughter Holly had accompanied me because she was the guest music artist at the conference where I was speaking. The phone rang. It was the local pastor's wife, my new friend, Kathy. She wanted to take us sightseeing. I laughed to myself wondering which part of "blind" people do not understand. However, I did not want a little thing like my diminished eyesight to stifle our day of fun and adventure. Kathy continued, "I have a surprise for you. I want to take you somewhere today. Be ready in ten minutes!"

Soon, Kathy pulled up to my hotel in her jeep. She told us we were going off-roading. I was not really sure what she meant, but we buckled up and off we went to the magnificent White Sands of New Mexico.

At first, I thought the scene was a cruel joke to play on a blind woman, since there was plenty of beach sand but no ocean. The White Sands of New Mexico are just that—all sand, as far as the eye can see. Scientifically stated, it is the world's largest surface deposit of gypsum.

Gypsum is one of Earth's most common mineral compounds, but gypsum is rarely seen on the earth's surface because it dissolves easily in water. Maybe it was a good idea, after all, that there were no crashing waves. Gypsum, unlike normal sand, is cool to the touch. It reflects the sun and does not absorb the heat. How thoughtful of the Creator to place it in the desert!

Kathy described to me the brilliant blue sky, the towering sand dunes, the endless miles of fine white sand, the birds above, and the mountain range beyond us. Her vivid descriptions easily helped this blind woman see the marvel. About ten minutes into the wide-open space of the Sands, Kathy stopped her jeep and asked me, "Want to drive?"

"Are you serious? Of course!" came my immediate reply. I quickly got into the driver's seat. Holly went to the passenger's side and Kathy got in the back with her video camera running. Now buckled in tighter, Kathy gave me some instruction about her jeep. With blind trust she told me to put it in drive. Then she issued forth a compelling challenge: *"Let's make a memory!"*

We laughed like schoolgirls. Holly was the designated guide to tell me where I was going and when to turn. Honking my horn, I zoomed out onto the open range. Kathy told Holly to crank up the radio. With our windows down and the sunroof wide open, our off-roading excursion was in full gear. I used my turn signals from time to time, pretending to be in traffic, as I waved at all the imaginary people. We laughed harder. The wide-open spaces made me feel carefree. With Kathy's descriptive guidance, there seemed to be no end to the marvel of the White Sands. It was great to be driving again. Oh, how I had missed this luxury!

But my carefree frame of mind quickly turned to concern when I encountered a bump in the road. Only a visually impaired woman could ram right into a huge dune. At this point, my off-roading escapade literally went to a new level. I had managed to run up the side of a dune and was lodged in a mountain of sand. Frightened, I took my foot off the gas. As we sat, teetering on the side of the massive dune, Kathy yelled out gleefully, *"Gun it!"*

Now I was the one to blindly trust!

I put the pedal to the metal, and soon we were back on the sandy course, upright and free of danger. It was so much fun as we meandered all around the crystal expanse. What a thrill and gift to have such an adventurous, brave friend.

Off-roading can be exhilarating, but when the driver is blindfolded, it's crazy. You have to be dependent on what others see and where they guide you. Fortunately, in the case of the White Sands, there was only one main entrance, which helped to safely contain our zany adventure. Our joyride was of our own making, without a planned destination or need of road maps.

I wonder if people live the same way? A high percentage of people are not fully sure *where* they are going, let alone where they want to be. This puzzles me. How would they even know when they arrived? Hope needs a plan of action. Sitting around, hoping for a better day or career advancement, is wishful thinking. Hope accompanies courage, initiative and concerted effort.

Hope is available in all positions in life. Hope comforts the weary and stands with the fearful. It keeps pace with the dreamer and is the support system of true pioneers who actively pursue the dreams that most never realize. Hope is present at every season of life. Ironically, hope is even available to those who seem hopeless.

Faith, hope, and love are featured together in the scriptures and their harmonic value brightens the darkest corner. When all is stolen, hope still remains. Hope enables us to reach for the impossible; it stabilizes the uncertainties in life. Hope sees beyond today and is not afraid to start over. The timing or location of your life's present predicament may seem to signal that you are off course. Course correct. Hope points to a better way at the intersection of your confusion and your goals.

Jim Irwin, of the Apollo 15 mission, was the eighth man to walk on the moon. In one of his famous interviews he shared surprising insights he gained from the Apollo 15 space mission. Though it took years of preparation and training to execute NASA's intended goal, Irwin's assessment of the actual flight was a tad unnerving.

Jim said that at the time of the launch NASA basically threw the Apollo mission toward the moon. Lacking a specific, well-traveled path, the spaceship's trajectory was merely based on substantive theory. With the moon as their destination, the team of astronauts course-corrected every ten minutes in an attempt to align themselves for a successful arrival. On the moon they had a five-hundred-mile landing perimeter. Once they reached their destination, Jim stepped out of the space vehicle and realized they had managed to land only five or ten feet *inside the boundary* of their landing perimeter. Talk about a close call!

If NASA, with all their Ph.D.'s in physics and aeronautics can allow for a little off-roading with the noble purpose of exploring new frontiers, can't you try to take a few new steps toward *your* dreams? The mission is not aborted if you have to course-correct along the way. Keep going.

Perfectly predictable living is unlikely. Life's uncertainties remove guarantees. But this doesn't mean established goals are without merit or that our efforts toward accomplishing those goals are without value.

What do you fear most? Hope offers real answers and is a fearless companion to dreamers. What do you wish for most often? Hope is willing to try to attain it through your efforts. What do you regret? Hope offers a new perspective and helps redeem any loss. What ties you up with no way of escape? Hope holds the key. What is the darkest hour of your life? Hope sees the turnaround and points to the dawn of a new day.

Hope sees what you cannot. Hope sees what you have overlooked. Hope sees beyond your limitations. Hope eases you back onto the path when you veer off course. Off-roading is fun for a season but not ideal for your life-long journey. Let hope pave the way for you.

Our youngest daughter, Lydia, spent a year overseas working with a mission outreach. Six months were spent in Germany and three months were spent in Liberia. Since she was a young girl she has always had a global interest, and she is fearless. During her time in Liberia the team of seven moved from their post in Chocolate City, outside the capitol city of Monrovia, to the jungle of Liberia, which is Cape Mount. The place she lived in was called the Evil Forest. The team's housing was primitive and their meals were slim. Often their work required them to walk to surrounding villages; the closest was one hour away.

Once when the team visited a small village, the younger children wanted to show the team the soccer field they had created. It was located deep in the jungle. Lydia was led into the forest by a young child who held her hand. Deeper into the jungle Lydia let go of his hand because the path was too narrow. She wanted him to walk in front of her on the dirt path because he was barefoot and there were thorns and thistles on the jungle floor. But he would not let go of her hand.

The young child extended his hand to Lydia to steady her on the path. This act of selfless concern still brings tears to think our daughter was kept safe far from our reach. The scene also reminds me of the willingness of hope to take our hand and steady us on uncertain paths.

There is no road or course you travel where hope does not reach to steady you. There is no reason to fear a narrow path, especially when hope walks with you. You do not walk alone.

CHAPTER FIFTEEN

B & B

*Hope never dies, but sometimes it
needs to be resuscitated.*

Typically, when I travel I stay in hotels, except on those rare occasions when a bed and breakfast has been offered. Though they may be unique in design and atmosphere, based on my experience I would not rate them as the most predictable environments. Perhaps this is why many love them. During our first experience in this homey type of lodging, my husband was napping in the afternoon when the feeling of being watched pulled him from a much-needed rest. As he slowly opened his eyes, he was startled to see a four-year-old looking right at him, and the little boy wasn't one of our own. He was the child of another guest family, and he had gone exploring. I have been wary of the whole B&B mystique ever since. Then, a few years later I learned it could get worse.

Much worse.

Tony and I had traveled to rural Alabama. Endless miles of moss covered trees, picturesque country roads, and swamplands surrounded us. In short, we were enshrouded in the Deep South. My host organization had arranged for us to stay at an award-winning B&B in the general region of my speaking engagement. This historic home was renowned for its great food and was furnished with priceless antiques. Our hosts were so excited to provide this place of peaceful repose.

Our forewarning of things to come might have been the roadblock by the Alabama State Highway Patrol on the night we arrived. There were makeshift roadblocks on the isolated, two-lane country road about ten miles from the B&B. As we pulled to a complete stop, Tony rolled down his window, and the patrolman shined his bright flashlight into our car. Tony asked the officer, "Is there a problem, sir?"

The patrolman leaned his head through the open window and took a good hard look at us. With a slow Southern drawl, he asked, "Where you folks from, anyway?" Then he seemed to slyly add, "You see, we kinda like to *know* who's visiting our neck of the woods."

Tony told him who we were and that I was speaking that week for a local event. Yet, the officer probed further. "Whereabouts are you staying *tonight*?"

We told him, and then he said, "You might want to consider another B&B. One in the *opposite* direction."

Puzzled, Tony explained the pre-arranged plans which seemed to satisfy both the officer and my husband, but not me. What on earth and *who* on earth was the officer looking for anyway? It was beginning to feel a little creepy. Not knowing the reason for the roadblock and this interrogation, my thoughts raced ahead, filling my mind with vivid imagery of every Hollywood cliché about the Deep South. I could picture it all so clearly. I projected escaped convicts; bloodhounds nosing their way through tall grass; and a posse of armed men wading knee-deep in alligator-infested swamps. A cold chill went over me. Finally, we were on our wary way and spent a restless night in the acclaimed country B&B. Oddly, we never learned why the roadblocks had been in place.

Due to a mix-up of overbooked reservations, we were informed that our time in the area would be split between two B&B's. So, we packed our bags and drove back into town where I spoke at the community gala. We were given room keys and informed we would be the only guests residing there. Afterward, we were directed to our new bed and breakfast. We were told the house was large, quaint, and quiet. I was relieved it was in the center of town. Exhausted, we looked forward to our new accommodations, and that we would be the only ones staying there. Imagine our shock when we pulled up to the curb and discovered that the B&B doubled as the local funeral home. No wonder it had a reputation for being a restful place. I guess you could say that it was our stay in that second inn that really put the nails in the coffin of the whole B&B experience!

A wrap-around porch with rockers welcomed us. The large dining room and kitchen were inviting. Our bedroom might have been considered luxurious in any other setting, but for some reason I wanted to rest with my eyes open and keep my shoes on. Until bedtime I was more comfortable sitting on the porch watching passersby than staying inside a quiet funeral home, waiting. My vivid imagination kept getting the best of me, and no words comforted me. I pled with Tony, "*Please* read me a chapter out of the Bible," Surely, I thought, it will calm my jitters. Tony chose Psalm 23, of course. "Though I walk through the valley of the shadow of death I will fear no evil." I hoped my eulogy would not be his next selected reading.

Unbeknownst to me, my husband was on pins and needles for a different reason. With my limited eyesight I hadn't noticed that our room was filled with knickknacks and breakable trinkets galore, including an assortment of figurines, vases, small picture frames and statues. Even our bathroom had glass statuettes and breakable items. Tony was uneasy about the possibility of my not seeing them and knocking something over or breaking one of the many items. I was oblivious to his stress.

Meanwhile, I asked Tony if there was a newspaper within reach, as I had the sudden urge to check the obituaries. If anyone else was coming in the middle of the night I wanted advance warning. Tony, trying to make light of all of it, said, "We won't be here long." Each quip of warped humor got worse.

Half-seriously, I begged, "Can you keep the lights on?" Tony playfully stated, "I hope you rest well tonight." In this spooky setting, those words suddenly felt like a grave finality. Instead of resting, I wanted to get up and dance around the room and make lots of noise. Some places in life are just too quiet. What perplexed me the most was wondering if we should lock the door. And, why did it matter? We were the sole occupants for the night. Who was I hoping to keep out?

"This too shall pass" was of no consolation as I reflected on my life. I started to soul search and confess all my sins under my breath. I could not imagine what was for breakfast or who would prepare it. Morning could not come soon enough. Surely you've noticed how some folks speak easily of death and mortality, while maintaining a hopeful outlook; others avoid the topic like the plague. Why is that?

An honest look at the brevity of life is essential—even healthy. Death is rarely welcome. It feels more harsh and unkind when young lives are cut short, but when you love someone, this life never gives us enough time to enjoy them. Those who are wise understand life as a mere vapor. How can anyone's hopes and dreams possibly be contained within a mere lifetime? Surely we are designed for more!

The only way to live this life in peace and without fear is to have a hope beyond this life. Hope springs eternal. I have no fear of death but dread the thought of wasting precious moments in this life. Too many folks walk around like zombies, void of any hope. I heard it said that most die full of ideas, inventions, plans and unfinished projects—if they have even started at all. Shouldn't the prize be to live life fully and rob the grave of all you possess within you now? Your dreams are not dead. Your grand plans still have life. Hope still is alive. Let it revive you and dream big once more.

Your life is not hopeless. Life's disappointments may have temporarily robbed your hope, but setbacks and shattered dreams do not have the power to dictate your future. It's never too late for a new beginning. Hope never dies, but sometimes it needs to be resuscitated.

No matter the life you live, it has a non-negotiable expiration date. Knowing this, shouldn't you value each day more and live it on purpose with purpose? To know there is life after this one is a comfort to me. But I embrace the value of choosing to live life now. What lies beyond this life is a gift, but not all have that assurance. Once you muster the courage to face your mortality head-on, you will finally be free to truly live *this* life. The optimum is living a life of hope.

Minutes turn to hours and hours to months. Before long, years accumulate. It is all very fleeting, so maximize the moments you have today and be totally alive.

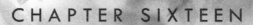

CHAPTER SIXTEEN

CURBSIDE

*Hope reveals treasures at the
curbside of your day's agenda.*

Have you ever found a treasure at the curbside? On certain days of the month, in different regions of the country, you are permitted to throw out large pieces of furniture and appliances. Some residents take this opportunity to drive by the night before and redeem items they can use. It might sound uncouth, but those who have a scout's eye have discovered some really nice items among the curbside discards. One man's trash is another's treasure.

In sharp contrast to taking items meant for the trash, Brenda, my generous friend in Michigan, decided to *leave* a gift at the curb for her garbage collection workers. It was a few days before Christmas and she wanted to thank them for their services. Brenda wrapped the gift and placed it on top of her garbage can. She watched from the upstairs window when the city sanitation truck came by on their rounds. Unaccustomed to receiving gifts in this manner and oblivious to the curbside treasure, in one swoop, the garbage man took the garbage can, with the wrapped present and all, and crushed them both in his dump truck. Oh well. It's the thought that counts, right?

Once I found a priceless gift on the curb of one of the busiest airports in the U.S. We were in a time crunch when we arrived at Orlando airport to fly back to Dallas. The lines were long, and Tony still needed to return the rental car. It looked impossible to manage the long lines unless I was dropped off to tackle them on my own. I was hesitant since I wondered how I would know when the line was moving and where, exactly, to go. Yet I agreed to try. Some adventures are more fun than others, but this one put my stomach in knots. Tony unloaded the luggage and strung our suitcases together so I could push them to the counter. If the queue had been a simple straight line I wouldn't have stressed about it, but the challenge was working my way through the line's maze. My only hope would be to make friends with the person in front of me and ask for help. This is always humbling and requires courage, but I was willing to do what it took to get the job done. Just as Tony was placing me in the long line, a woman cut in front of me to go first. Tony hugged me goodbye. Our plan was to meet at the gate beyond security. I would ask for assistance once at the counter, but it would be awhile getting there.

Assessing the situation with everything literally in a blur, I said to the person in front of me, "Hi! My name is Gail. Could you help me?"

The lady in front of me proved to be both pleasant and willing. "My name is Genia," she politely offered.

I told her my dilemma. "I lost my eyesight and need you to please tell me when the line moves."

We both agreed that she would simply tug at my luggage when the line moved forward, and I would follow her lead. It sounded doable. Genia was easy to talk to and our conversation was fun and rich. We quickly discovered that we had similar passions in life. Our interests included family, work, people and both of us were Christians.

I told her I was from Dallas and asked where she was from. She said her home was in North Carolina and her visit to Orlando came at the last minute. Then Genia confessed that she had actually been in line inside the terminal when she felt prompted to go outside to get in line instead. On her way to the line outside of the building she saw Tony helping me, so she darted to get ahead of me to save some time. We laughed together since now she was stuck with me. I asked Genia questions about her family, and she asked about mine. When I told her my story, she was visibly moved.

While talking about her oldest son, Genia mentioned he was working in the Los Angeles area with a film producer. Surprised by another coincidence in our life paths, I said I also had a friend in the film industry. In fact, he lives in Hawaii but works often in L.A. Then I said his name.

Genia exclaimed, "My son works with him!"

I pulled out my phone to text my film friend to let him know either he was famous or, "it's a small world after all," which seemed appropriate for the location we found ourselves in. Next, I learned about Genia's second son who was adopted from Liberia.

"No way!" I said with laughter. "Our youngest daughter worked in Liberia last year with orphans."

Genia then told me of her daughter, Anna.

"Are you kidding? We have a daughter named Anna."

Our continued conversation revealed one common thread after another, and the design of this tapestry was beautiful.

I'm not sure if the line moved fast or if our conversation made it appear to, but there seemed to be no end to the surprises I discovered in this curbside treasure. By the time we reached the ticket counter, we had exchanged numbers and knew we would be friends for life.

Genia lingered as I got my ticket in order, then we walked together to security. I am not sure what short line Tony found, but he met up with us at security. There the three of us talked fast as we repeated for Tony's benefit all the surprises of finding one another. Making myself vulnerable to a complete stranger had given me a once-in-a-lifetime opportunity to find a curbside treasure.

After we three were separated for a short time while each one of us went through the security check points, we picked right back up and walked to our gates. They were right next to each other. I reached into my bag to give Genia a gift. I happened to have a copy of my autobiography, *Seeing Beyond*, with me. I quickly signed it before handing it to her. When Genia saw its title, she started to cry. Sensing my puzzlement, she hugged me goodbye and said, "One day I will explain." On that note, we said our final farewell.

Later in the week I received an email from Genia. She wrote that she was amazed how we met and confirmed our new friendship. She told me about her desire to write a book one day and tell her own story. She shared with me that a title she loved was "Seeing Beyond," because her life message included a call to look beyond circumstances, and she wondered if someone already had the title. When she specifically researched it online several weeks previously she said, "Shoot! Someone has that title." The title in question, of course, was my own—thus the tears at the airport when I handed her my book. Until that moment she had doubted her adequacy to write, but now on a curb in a city neither of us lived in and through uncanny circumstances, she found new encouragement to move forward with her writing project.

Looking back on that fateful day, my focus could have been my disability and the long line of inconvenience. Instead, by finding the courage to ask a complete stranger for help, I made a life-long friend. Tony and I have visited Genia and her husband several times in the Carolinas. No one would guess we have known each other for only a short time. We still laugh at the way in which we met—and marvel at God's sense of humor.

I sometimes wonder if I have missed making other precious friends as I've trudged along my life's way, consumed in my own world and with my pressing schedule. I wonder if some interruptions are blessings in disguise, sent my way intentionally so I can discover more of life's hidden treasures. Why don't you try it? Train yourself to see beyond the delays and look for what surprises await you. It seems that I meet the most interesting people when I'm "on my way" to do something else!

A few weeks ago we were on a plane that was delayed on the tarmac for over an hour. The cargo crew reported a potentially dangerous concern with one of the tires. While we were stuck there, I struck up a conversation with the passenger next to me. In the short amount of time we talked about our careers and exchanged stories and names. She plans to contact me to speak to her company. Crazier still, we all had to get off the aborted flight and board separate planes in order to reach our designated cities. My seatmate ended up having to change airlines. We would never have met had it not been for the seeming inconvenience of a bum tire!

Dare to believe that nothing happens purely by accident, and don't lose hope. It has a very practical way of helping all things work for our good. Hope reveals treasures cleverly disguised at the curbside of your day's agenda.

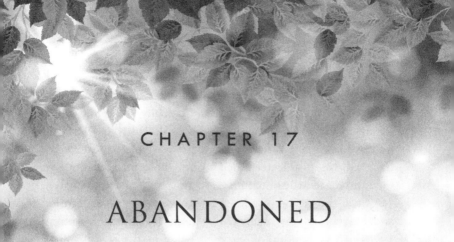

CHAPTER 17

ABANDONED

Hope will never abandon you.

Over the years, I have been called an Ambassador of Hope. I love that title. The desires to encourage, motivate and inspire my fellow man are in my DNA. Yet, I wish for something more to say to help throw out a lifeline to those who struggle to overcome abandonment.

A young married woman fell into deep despair when her hopes for her marriage were shattered by infidelity. Her husband's unfaithfulness left her unable to cope. Betrayal left a near fatal wound that would not stop the hemorrhaging of her heart. Impostors, posing as friends, betrayed her, too, with their gossip and rejection. It hurt to breathe. She quit eating as her desire to live waned. She stopped answering her phone and ignored the doorbell.

Many days passed.

Then, a persistent friend who genuinely cared barged through her door, determined to help and protect. She fed her distraught friend crackers until she could lift her head again. Her friend's strength returned and, gradually, she found a new reason to live. In time, with the aid of skilled counselors and prayer, her trust was restored and she was able to forgive her husband. She was determined to be whole through hope in God, no matter the outcome.

Over the period of a few years, her marriage was restored and her family was rescued. Her hope for a new beginning started with a handful of crackers. True friendship, in its most obstinate form, is often the only lifeline a desperate person has in their struggle to choose life.

Another friend of mine battled much longer with betrayal. Late one afternoon Jan returned home from teaching school. Her two young boys followed her into the house that lay in the wooded plains near the riverbank. It was half past four. Her husband was normally already home by this time, so she wondered where he could be. Her husband had left for work earlier than usual that morning, and now he was also delayed in coming home. In her heart Jan knew something wasn't adding up.

She quieted her anxieties by thinking about dinner preparations for their evening meal. Scurrying around the kitchen, she said aloud, "Where is that man of mine?" Their mutual agreement was to notify one another if they were ever going to be late, but he hadn't called. Trying to stay calm, she mentally reviewed their goodbyes that morning. Her husband had simply kissed her and said he was going to work earlier than usual so he could get his truck's radiator fixed before clocking in.

The fears of patterns of the past now crowded her mind. She battled to suppress the memories of former painful days when on occasion, he would be gone at random times from their home with no explanation or excuses. Those days seemed like a distant past, because it had been three years since it had happened. To quiet her fears Jan went to look at her husband's closet to see if anything was missing, but all was normal and in place.

Her husband had sustained an injury while on the job, but he still worked for the company. Days earlier, his long awaited medical settlement had finally arrived. Their future plans of buying acreage were now within their grasp. Though long-overdue dreams were about to come true, the past few months had been riddled with depression. The whole family had been on pins and needles during times of dealing with his injury.

Jan's husband was a kind southern gentleman who was liked by everyone. No one knew of his history. But Jan remembered all too well the last time he had disappeared. He had gone on a drinking binge to the Gulf of Mexico with no one knowing his whereabouts until he returned three months later. He had spent their household funds on his escapade, and when he returned even his wedding ring was missing. He claimed to have no memory of what he had done. He never divulged the secrets of where he had been.

Jan had learned, over the span of her ten-year marriage, to depend on faith and set her heart on the Lord. She delighted in her sons and their home. Her forgiving ways and steadfast love anchored their family. Her constant joy and enthusiasm for life remained unchanged through it all. But, at this moment, fear gripped her heart as she wondered why her husband still hadn't come home.

Jan called her husband's supervisor to ask what time her husband had left work. The supervisor confirmed Jan's deepest fear with his reply. "He did not come to work today." Her throat went dry. In her heart, Jan feared her husband had abandoned his family again. Dreams now threatened to be nightmares as a wife and two sons were suddenly abandoned. Jan determined to search for answers and every clue was important. Was he even alive? She had to know.

Next, Jan picked up the phone and called me. She calmly stated her concern. "Gail, I have reason to believe that my husband is missing. Would you pray with me?"

Jan and her family were in the church my husband pastored and Jan taught at our private school where her sons were enrolled. They had been actively involved and would do anything for anyone. Through the years God had brought healing to their home.

After a long, sleepless night, Jan's phone rang once again. Jan quickly reached for the phone. It was the mechanic. "Ma'am. I just wanted to say your husband left his thermos at our shop yesterday. I thought you might want to know." Around town, word of the missing man spread quickly. Prayer vigils were organized, while other concerned friends donated meals to Jan and her boys.

Every day the search continued with phone calls, meetings with the police and interviews with local media. Townspeople prayed fervently for a helpful lead to develop. Jan's hope and faith strengthened her young family, yet the signs of stress were evident on the boys' faces. They feared they had done something wrong that had caused their dad to leave them. The search for this missing husband and father was long and tedious. Every road led to another dead end. Meanwhile, Jan's household finances were in a state of ruin. Her husband had drained their bank accounts.

The shattered hearts of the three left behind was confusing and unexplainable. Her hope remained focused and her prayer consistent. "Lord, we place our trust in you." Her strength and complete trust stood firm. In prayer, Jan gladly practiced exchanging her current abandonment for the promise that God was protecting her. His words comforted her. She believed God's promise that He would never leave her or forsake her. Three months passed without a word from her husband. Then, Jan received another phone call.

The young woman introduced herself to Jan, using her full name. Then she announced, "I have reason to believe you are my mother-in-law. A prolonged and awkward silence occurred as the caller finished delivering the news. "I believe your husband is my husband's father."

Jan was stunned speechless. She could only listen as the caller continued. "Your husband left my husband's mother when she was pregnant. I am calling because my husband has a rare illness and we are trying to get information from his birth father. Can you help me?"

Shocked by this possibility, Jan asked some questions. Was this woman legitimate? Or had she dialed the wrong number?

Before divulging her concerns, Jan first needed more clarification. The young woman's facts were accurate and the stories she relayed were mystifying. Soon, Jan knew the caller was legitimate. Jan began to tell her that the man she was looking for had disappeared from their lives as well.

Jan's husband was an impostor and a polygamist. This missing "husband" had spent years spinning a web of deception and entangled in it were a string of innocent women and their unsuspecting offspring. He had never divorced any of his previous wives, and it was unclear how many wives he actually had. The young lady asked Jan's permission to continue her search. Jan agreed and asked if they would let her know what she discovered.

Three years passed before Jan and her sons learned where the boys' father had gone: he was living in another state, remarried with yet another family. Jan never lost her faith as she faithfully raised her family. Her sons are now young men, and Jan has recently remarried.

The power of prayer and her constant hope provided Jan the emotional footing to weather life's storms. I know similar heartbreaking stories of betrayal, experienced not only by wives, but also by husbands and children. The same empowering hope is available to all. If you, or someone you love, are reeling from the long-term effects of betrayal, you can be confident that hope will never abandon you. You are loved with a steadfast love.

A nameless little baby lay hungry and in danger under a tree in Uganda. Abandoned, he was too young to hope himself, but hope came just the same. A surprised woman happened upon the babe and gave him his name, Mumwata. It was the Ugandan word for "trash." Can you imagine the hopelessness built in to such a name?

Growing up in the village, this precious little boy was called trash by everyone. Meanwhile, on the other side of the world, a Christian couple and their three young children were praying for God to use their lives. He placed adoption on their hearts but gave no clear direction as to who or when. As an act of faith, they went to a vacant bedroom in their house. They asked God to fill it.

Nine months later and countless costly trials in the complicated world of international adoption, Holly and Bradley adopted two young children from Uganda to be part of their family. Each child was given a new legal name. James William, formerly "trash," was also given a new African name, Akanonda, which means, "God has chosen me."

Hope finds you even if you exist half-obscured in the deep brushes of life, and renames you. Hope fills an empty life with purpose. Hope rescues the abandoned. Hope calms the fears of previous loss. Hope in the promise that He will never leave you or forsake you.

CHAPTER EIGHTEEN

LIVE

Hope will give you a will to live.

One October it was time for a new battery to be installed in my pacemaker. It is a sobering reality to know that one little box and a ten-year battery keep me ticking, but I *am* grateful my pacemaker keeps a spring in my step.

Ten days after the surgery, I returned to the heart clinic to have the bandages removed and my pacemaker checked. I view these routine service calls as necessary inconveniences in my quest for longevity. I listened for my name to be called. It was a crowded waiting room of my busy cardiologist.

"Gail McWilliams" came the loud robotic voice of the male nurse. With his monotonic intonation, the nurse slowly moved the line of patients closer to the examination rooms.

"Hey! I remember you from last time," I said cheerfully to the backside of my male nurse as he led me down the hallway. I had to ask, "What is your name again?"

"John with an 'h'." We chatted a bit before John pointed ahead, instructing me with no emotion, "To the scales you go."

Dreading what the scales would reveal, I said: "John, this is where we part ways as friends!"

John steadied my arm as I kicked off my shoes. When I realized he was not going to release his firm grip, I looked at John and scolded, "Take your hand off me!"

Shocked by my demand, John quickly stepped back. He mentally sifted through my directive, wondering if he should be offended. Then, smiling, I continued, "Your hand may add extra weight."

Chuckling aloud, John announced for all to hear, "Great! We have a comedian in the house today."

In the examining room, electrodes were adhered to my rib cage and chest wall, and the tests were under way. After my pacemaker's new battery had been thoroughly monitored, the nurse announced, "Your battery should be good for another nine years."

"What?" I protested. "I thought a ten-year battery was placed in my chest. How have I lost one full year in two short weeks?" I felt like a new automobile that had just pulled away from the car dealership, depreciating thousands of dollars while signaling to merge back onto the street. I quipped, "I better get to living life fast!"

Are plans for living a full life included on your calendar of events? Or have you postponed your hopes for another day?

My Dad once sustained quite a psychological shock when he went to his hometown in Missouri to attend his uncle's funeral. When my parents arrived at the funeral home, Dad's own name was on the marquee. You see, Dad was the namesake of this uncle. In fact, the service seemed so personalized that Dad later reported he felt as if he had attended his own funeral.

Both men had similar life experiences. The officiating pastor talked about Uncle Chet's love for his family, his service in the U.S. Navy, and his strong work ethic. He also mentioned that Chet was a good and decent man. Dad hoped the same would be said in his own eulogy, one distant day. Dad tried to concentrate on the minister's comforting words but his focus kept returning to the brevity of life.

Dad is an engineer and has always had a propensity for mathematics. With his thoughts fixated on his own mortality, he began to mentally calculate, "in God minutes," just how much time remained on his cosmic clock. Dad based his calculations on two verses of scripture. "With the Lord one day is like a thousand years…" 2 Peter 3:8, and, "The days of our lives are seventy years; and if by reason of strength they are eighty years" Psalm 90:10. Applying these mysterious calculations to his current age, Dad somehow figured he only had about twelve more minutes to live!

Some might call it a coincidence that, since attending his own funeral, my Dad has written and published four books and his fifth is in the works. And, he wrote them all while recuperating from a near fatal heart condition, known simply as The Widow Maker.

What about your own journey? Are you making the most of every moment? I once heard a man say he was not afraid of death. His only fear was facing death before he had truly lived. I believe it is possible to continue living a hope-filled life even when faced with a grave diagnosis. I am grateful to have several friends who beat the odds when it comes to an incurable disease. Each of them is focused on living and not on the grim disease itself.

One such story is my friend from Pennsylvania. Tim was just eighteen when he finished his freshman year in college. When his family picked him up from school, he complained of exhaustion, blaming it on his demanding workload. Thankfully, Tim's grandmother was a nurse. One look at Tim and she knew the culprit threatening his health was much more than exhaustion.

Tim's family doctor ordered a vast array of blood tests. Then, when all the results were gathered, Tim and his parents were called in for a conference. There, the doctor explained that all three of Tim's blood counts were alarming: Tim had severe aplastic anemia and was not expected to live to be nineteen. This disease is the deadly result of damaged bone marrow that can neither produce new red and white blood cells nor platelets.

One day a medical resident visited Tim at his bedside, concerned that he had not grasped the terminal nature of his disease. This young doctor wanted to make sure Tim understood the severity of his disease and that he only had a few months to live. It seems that Tim was too much at peace for the resident's comfort. Exasperated he said, "You do realize this is a death sentence, don't you? Why doesn't your attitude reflect that?"

Tim quickly responded, "I know you guys have told me when I'm going to die. But, you could walk out of this hospital right now and get hit by a car and be dead. The way I look at it, I have an advantage over you, I know what you think is going to happen to me, but you don't know when your own time is going to be over."

Before he left the hospital, Tim made a decision. Despite the doctor's prognosis, he planned to *live*. Tim transferred to a local college and arranged for his brother to act as his proxy when his transfusion schedule, or physical weakness, caused him to miss class.

Overnight, Tim left the carefree life of a typical teen-aged boy behind and assumed full responsibility for his life as an adult. He wisely made some health changes and focused on living his life to the fullest, in spite of the inconvenience of relentless blood tests to monitor his "demise."

Two months later, test results stunned the doctors. Tim's blood counts were improving! Very slowly, but steadily, his blood cell counts continued to resume healthier levels. Then, another health crisis ensued.

Seven years later on Christmas Day, Tim was diagnosed with paroxysmal nocturnal hemoglobinuria (PNH), another rare but related blood disorder. Tim was given a second death sentence when his doctor informed him that PNH is also fatal. The unusual name of this disease is derived from its symptoms that are most severe at night when the blood cells prematurely break down and systematically overwhelm the body. Tim told me this description is misleading because the blood cells are constantly breaking down.

After years of blood infusions, and in spite of multiple clots, Tim has long outlived the doctors' prognosis. His counts have once again returned to normal without treatment. Miraculously, he has never undergone a bone marrow transplant. And what about Tim's influence on that young resident doctor? He is currently a Family Practice Physician and he still sees Tim from time to time.

Tim recently turned fifty and continues to live a very active, healthy life. Tim manages a radio network in Pennsylvania that extends hope to thousands of daily listeners. His wife and three daughters work with him to share the good news that hope lives.

My cousin Carla is in the battle for her life. Five years ago she was diagnosed with Leiomyosarcoma, a rare, terminal cancer that attacks the soft tissues of the body. Tumors currently affect twelve areas of Carla's body, including her liver, lungs, legs, her spine and near her heart. At the cellular level, the tentacles of these tumors continue to spread throughout her body, resulting in chronic pain.

She will not give up on living. Carla's drive to live and her hope are amazing to observe. She disdains pity. Her vision for her future is in the forefront of her thoughts and her life goals seem unending. She is notably reluctant to discuss her health issues in casual conversation. In fact, Carla is so practiced in her concern for others that she quickly refocuses her attention back on those inquiring about her health. You must be persistent if you hope to pry out of her any updates on her medical status.

Carla actively cooperates with the specialists who have committed themselves to researching her illness. She is open to new treatment methods and hopes for a cure to this horrible disease, even if it doesn't manifest itself in her lifetime. Carla's doctors privately moan as they review her chart notes before entering the examination room. They must wrestle with their feelings of helplessness, realizing they have no medically validated hope to offer their dear patient. Then, they enter the exam room where Carla greets them with pleasantries and a smile. The doctors are surprised and say, "Well, you actually look pretty good compared to what is on paper."

Recently, an oncologist asked Carla a daunting question after reviewing her records and identifying multiple organs with serious infiltration. Impacted by Carla's debilitating cancer, her multiple surgeries and her ongoing treatment, he addressed the elephant in the room.

"Carla. Do you still want to keep fighting?"

Taking a nanosecond to ponder his question, Carla sweetly replied, "My kidneys are still good. Let's keep going."

Carla deliberately chooses to remain focused on others in the midst of her mounting pain. She has sustained at least five bone fractures, she has difficulty walking, and often her breathing is shallow. Yet Carla radiates an uncommon, abiding joy. She is steadfast in her positive outlook and is truly grateful for all God has given her. My amazing cousin lives in constant physical pain but continually marinates her soul in hope.

Though Carla's prognosis is grim, she has already lived three years beyond her projected life. In spite of everything, she still drives and only occasionally uses a wheelchair at the airport when she flies out of state for more scans and treatments. Through it all, she is pleasant, determined and fully alive.

Tim, Carla, and my Dad are each beating the odds by living hope-infused lives. No matter the outcome of any of their stories, their choice to live life intentionally enables Hope to saturate each of their remaining days. Many face far less physical traumas in life, yet wallow in self-pity as they struggle to find reason to go on living. More tragic are those who are content to merely exist, yet they have never fully lived.

I believe hope will give you a will to live. Go on, *Live!*

CHAPTER NINETEEN

DECISIONS

*Decide to make Hope part
of your life.*

For several years I have hosted my own national radio program. One of the perks associated with a career in broadcasting is attending the convention of National Religious Broadcasters (NRB). Here, fellow hosts, program directors, and network owners join top innovative producers and filmmakers from every imaginable branch of broadcasting for five days steeped in professional opportunities. Within the NRB's training workshops, keynote addresses from inspirational speakers, and performances by wonderful entertainers, lies a vast network of rich friendships, both old and new.

One year I invited our daughter, Lindey, to join us. Lindey had been busy with two little boys and a household in transition. This convention would be a nice diversion and time away for retrospection. When we arrived, the beautiful Gaylord Opryland Hotel and Convention Center in Nashville was overrun with NRB conferees. Multitudes of broadcasting vendors were spread throughout this lavish venue. Each person in attendance filled their personal agenda to maximize media expansion for the coming year.

Among my list of elective meetings and receptions, I had reserved time for reunions with my list of favorite friends. One was with my dear friend, Joni Eareckson Tada. Joni's personal story is one bathed in God's amazing grace. Her faith, coupled with hope, continues to influence people worldwide.

Joni was an active, athletic youth who loved horseback riding and swimming. One outing that should have been some fun with friends resulted in horror. She dove into the Chesapeake Bay, unaware of the shallow waters, due to the changing tide. She felt a shock go through her body. Her sister swam to assist Joni when she saw her body float lifelessly to the water's surface. It soon became apparent that Joni had suffered a severe spinal cord injury.

Joni remembers when her sister retrieved her that her arms had no feeling. Joni naively thought this uncomfortable sensation would only last for a short time. But in the twinkling of an eye, Joni had gone from an athletic young teen to a quadriplegic, paralyzed from her shoulders down.

Joni could not imagine a life imprisoned in a wheelchair. The world of immobility was foreign to this fresh young life. She struggled with depression and anger as she wrestled with life's most haunting questions. Joni shared, "I sought to find a final escape, a final solution, through assisted suicide, begging my friends to slit my wrists, dump pills down my throat, *anything* to end my misery. The source of my depression was understandable. I could not face the prospect of sitting down for the rest of my life without the use of my hands, without the use of my legs. All my hopes seem dashed."

Joni struggled for two long, dark years with her fists tightly clenched and relentlessly asking unanswerable questions in a tone of anger. Joni candidly shares, "I was sick and tired of pious platitudes that well-meaning friends often gave me at my bedside. Patting me on the head, trivializing my plight, with the sixteen good biblical reasons as to why all this had happened. I was tired of advice and didn't want any more counsel. I was emotionally numb, desperately alone, and so very, very frightened."

Only God could redeem such loss and restore joy and purpose in the midst of such a profound tragedy. With help from a faithful Bible-believing friend, Joni's tightly clenched fists gradually turned into open hands, willing to be used for God's work in her unique situation.

Joni is a beloved author and speaker, as well as an accomplished artist and recording vocalist. She has advised presidents and is an advocate for the disabled. Her ministry, *Joni and Friends,* has reached around the globe with practical help and extended hope to those in need of a lifeline.

During one of Joni's subsequent physical challenges, as she lay flat on her back to help heal some pressure sores on her body, two gentlemen visited Joni to propose an idea. They thought Joni should have a radio show to share her faith and hope with others. Joni's initial response was filled with the concern that she would run out of things to say within the first two weeks. Joni's decision to accept the ministry challenge birthed a radio show that today—some thirty-five years later—has spread across the nation. I know Joni still has more to say. *Joni and Friends* appeals to all, no matter where members of her listening audience find themselves. From the onset of our friendship, I have loved referring to us as "Joni and her McFriend."

Joni's compelling story is outlined in her autobiography and was featured on the silver screen. This film was a favorite for our children, especially Lindey. I always say Joni runs circles around everyone else. She laughs and claims that I see more keenly than anyone else. We make quite a pair. Each of us is blessed with a husband who possesses the uncommon strength of character to serve his wife with loyalty and patient love. When the four of us are together, Joni and I sit and talk at one end of the table while our husbands sit and listen at the other end, most likely enjoying the reprieve.

This particular year, Lindey joined me to connect with Joni at one of the coffee shops in our hotel. Lindey sat at the left of Joni, and I was seated on her right. Our coffee was served while we talked fast and furious.

"Lindey, would you please help me get a drink of coffee?" came Joni's humble request.

Lindey later confessed she was a bit star struck. She quickly lifted the cup of steaming coffee to Joni's mouth.

Without missing a beat, Joni and I carried on our delightful conversation, updating each other on the events of the past year. We laughed and shared our insights and challenges within the framework of exchanged stories. Joni is a skilled listener and her thoughtful questions hint openly of her profound insights and intentional approach to living a purpose-filled life. Plus, she is a great audience for my new stories.

The idea for this very book is a result of one of the coffees Joni and I shared the first time we ever met. She enthusiastically commissioned me by saying, "Gail, you must write a book and tell us what you see." Joni and I share unique lives and we love to inspire others. Both of us know all too well that God has been good to us. Lindey expressed later that she was in awe. I'm sure anyone watching observed a unique scene with Lindey offering Joni sips of coffee and helping me to know where my cup was located.

My daughter's eyes welled with tears as she studied her subjects. To hear Lindey tell it, she sat watching two powerful women joyfully embracing each of their lives' costly assignments, oblivious to any sense of loss. The impact of that moment has a ripple effect on all of us to this day.

That day over coffee, Lindey resolutely decided that she could overcome any of life's challenges or disappointments. She had a full life to live that was dependent alone on her choice to believe. Lindey resolved to face each season of life and any change with intentional faith, knowing God's grace is sufficient. The bonus blessing at the table that day was something none of us knew—Lindey was pregnant with her third child, their first daughter. Windsor Hope was born eight months later. Windsor means "a turn in the river," and Hope is "the present gift." Throughout Windsor's life, Lindey's decision that fateful day will continue to influence untold future generations.

Joni captures the expectant essence of hope in her remarks. "I began to get a buoyant, lively hope of heavenly glories above. In other words, this wheelchair helped me to see that the good things in this life aren't the best things. There are better things yet to come."

Hope has your best interest at heart, so decide to embrace it at every opportunity. I remember Dad telling me in my teens, "You can have whatever you want, Gail. Just choose wisely." Life consists of a series of choices, and those choices have consequences. As children, we helplessly bore the consequences of our caregivers' decisions but the decisions we now face are ours to make. Embrace decision-making and invite hope into the process. My goal in writing this book is to help you see that hope is more than a mere wishful thought—hope is tailor-made for every situation. You alone must decide if you want it to empower you.

Some like to see the negative. Complaining and whining are two of their favorite hobbies. You get good at whatever you practice. In the past, our ancestors may have been hardwired for worry and fear, but going forward you can draw a line in the sand of their negativity and make it the start over point for future generations who see no limits.

You can live without hope, but it will age you. You can continue to woefully sing the blues, but when you decide to switch out your playlist, you will begin to hear songs of hope in the darkest places of your life. You will no longer need to wear the shabby garment of hopelessness, because hope travels with His own customized wardrobe. Hope is at the revolving door waiting patiently to deliver you from feelings of abandonment and isolation into a larger spiritual space filled with the comfort of assurance and peace.

Hope is well mannered and, therefore, will never force himself on you. He simply offers his arm to those who want to dance. Hope points out the answers, while those around you stumble to formulate their questions. Hope fosters a confident, decisive attitude and is the perfect accessory for success and personal fulfillment.

Hope for a child to fill your empty arms; Hope to pass your difficult test; Hope to be loved in the aftermath of neglect or abuse; Hope to find the job best suited for you and Hope for the home in which you have longed to live. All things are possible, if only you will believe. Do not grow weary and lose hope. There is hope in the midst of lack, as well as hope in abundance.

Prayer is a conduit of hope, bidding it to come near. Hope lends vision to your situation when your own eyes search for a way of escape. Hope is the perfect centerpiece for the corporate conference table to your own dining room table. Decide to make hope part of your life, no matter the present insufficiency. Make the decision to give hope a chance by actively guarding your thoughts and watching every word that proceeds from your mouth.

Make the decision to put hope in life's equation, and keep looking in a forward direction. If you're always glancing nervously in life's rear-view mirror, yesterday's disappointment will continue to rob you of tomorrow's promise. Refuse to allow past failures to gauge your future outcome. Make the decision, once and for all time, that success is within your reach. Practice hoping for the best and looking for what you may have missed or previously underestimated.

Won't you please join me in my blind trust that hope has a perfect work to do in each of our lives in ways that are beyond what we could ever imagine or dream. After all, and *through* it all,

Hope Sees.

CHAPTER TWENTY

PERSONAL

Hope is my best friend.

I love the subject of hope. Years ago I asked myself, "What would a blind woman do to prove she is a woman of hope?" Suddenly I thought of the answer. "She would put her car keys back into her purse."

So, I did!

I believe it is important to put something within your hand that is tangible and reminds you to hope again. For me, it was my car keys, and the hope that I would one day drive again. For you it may be something you lack, or long to see restored. It could be a picture of a child who appears lost. An old time key can remind you there are more of life's treasures to unlock. A silver pen could encourage you to author the book you have dreamed of writing. It might be a logo of a business you sketched on a dinner napkin, or a framed skyline of a city where you long to live. The point is, engage in hope.

My husband, Tony, has placed a picture of hungry children in front of us to remind us we can offer hope beyond our own zip code. Tony started a company while I was writing this book, called, "Hope Quest Global." It is part of a Hope Movement and implements social entrepreneurial ideas. He has also launched his first podcast to teach others how to impact their physical world. His interviews with a wide cross-section of social entrepreneurs present courageous solutions that will influence our culture.

Tony and I share a growing concern for the world's malnourished children. We want to give hope to those who cannot speak for themselves. We hope to make a difference with a cause bigger than our own needs and dreams.

Hope has never been just some wishful thought or wish list. Instead, hope is substance and the mortar of the building blocks of our lives. It is beauty to the tattered; it is comfort to the mourning; it is freedom to the shackled; it is refreshment to the wilted. Hope is gentle to the battered and a friend to the dejected. Hope is a path when you have lost your way, and a fortress when the enemy of your soul attacks your domain. Hope is the hand offered to help you get back up and sustains your strength so you can run life's race and finish your course well.

When I wrote about hope it was more than a thought. It was about a person. I wanted to introduce you to Hope—Jesus Christ. I fell more in love with Hope Himself while I wrote this book. I recognize this enduring quality of hope is needed in all of life's situations but is best seen and experienced in the very person of Jesus. I wanted you to see what I see.

In my darkest hours, the God of Comfort and Hope embraced me. I have had Hope sing over me in the night seasons. Hope has stood by my side when it felt like everyone abandoned me. Hope carved out a path in the most impossible situations while offering me a light along my way. Hope has never disappointed, even though I have tasted of life's disappointments. Hope has been my calm in the tumultuous storms and stabilized me in the uncertainties of my own life. Hope has strengthened my faith and nurtured my prayer life. Hope has absorbed the pain and deflected the worst of news. Hope has given me a new summit from which to see the bigger view.

Hope has always been there in my yesterdays, is active in my today and is ready for tomorrow, should it come. No matter the loss or the gain, Hope is there. Hope helped me dream as a child the very life I now lead.

Hope has kept me at the computer writing new resources, telling me not to stop until others are inspired. Hope has laughed with me when the bad news turns to good news. Hope has danced with me when the music lifts my spirit and gives me cause to celebrate every victory. Hope shared every season and, along with me, anticipated the next open door. Hope reminds me I have value, and nothing is impossible if I can believe.

Hope has never left my side, and to live without it, for me, is non-optional. Hope carried me when I was too tired to walk and lifted me out of valleys to the next high point of my life.

Hope has removed my blinders and washed the tears from my eyes.

Hope is present, yet eternal. Hope is my best friend.

I am not sure what you believe and why, but if you do not know the Hope I know, please let me introduce you to Him. There is a void in each of us that we try to fill. Ecclesiastes 3:11 states there is a longing for eternity in all our hearts. Yet we often try to fill this craving with everything but the perfect fit for our life. Each of us consists of spirit, soul and body. The spirit is the innermost part and can only be made alive by Hope Himself. The void can only be filled when the missing piece is placed into the eternity gap. To try to make a counterpart work goes against the very design of the Master Designer who knows you best. Jesus will never force Himself on us but waits for us to ask Him to make us complete and fill the vacuum.

From the beginning of time, mankind has faced a hopeless dilemma. The only solution meant sending God's only Son to die on our behalf, pardon our sin and free us to live in hope eternal. Consider what Hope sees. From the cross Jesus saw you and me and, in spite of our hopeless state, was brutally crucified, only to reestablish His hope on our lives. The followers of Jesus fell into deep despair. They had misunderstood heaven's purpose when Jesus experienced a cruel death, and Hope was buried. At the end of three days the Hope of the ages was raised from the dead. Consequently, Hope lives on and our lives have been changed forever.

Now, what will you do with Hope?

Only one could bridge the gap, and it was Hope Himself. Jesus gave His life to pardon ours and free us from the prison of sin we were in. His love forgave us a debt we could never pay. This resurrection gives new life and empowers us to live. This Hope had a plan long before the foundations of the earth, and that plan includes you. However, you will have to choose Hope for yourself. Just ask.

I gladly embrace my life's assignment to be an Ambassador of Hope. You can be one, too. Hope will give you the boost to see over and past what has obscured your view. Your life can now reflect a bright new focus.

And through it all, Hope Sees.

ACKNOWLEDGEMENTS

A special thanks to my hope team:

Linda McChesney Eisenmayer—Content strategist

Tonya Asekhauno—My assistant

Ryan Duckworth—Graphic consultant

Chet and Janet Moyers—Content consultants

Jill Hellwig—Encouraging McFriend

Bob Bubnis—Awesome designer

Bruce Barbour—Literary consultant

Thank you to all who let me share their stories so that others might hope again.

My deepest gratitude to Tony McWilliams who partners with me no matter the task, assignment or engagement—his love and support is constant. And, to our incredible children and grandchildren who give me hope for the next generation.

APPENDIX

Here is a short list of organizations where you might be able to find help and hope.

Foreword
  JoniAndFriends.org

Chapter Three
  DallasLighthouse.org
  FreedomScientific.com

Chapter Five
  Ziglar.com

Chapter Seven
  Mend.org
  AccidentalImpacts.org
  CompassionateFriends.org
  RoeverFoundation.org
  BrendaNevitt.com

Chapter Eight
  NewLifeSolutions.org/sols-story/
  InternationalHelpline.org
  Care-Net.org
  HeartbeatInternational.org
  SaveTheStorks.org
  EmbraceGrace.com
  RoeverFoundation.org
  HopeForTheHeart.org

Chapter Twelve
  DinaHackert.com
  FCA.org

Chapter Seventeen
  NobleCall.org
  MarriageToday.com
  FamilyTalk.org
  FaithBridgeFosterCare.org
  AWAA.org
  Bethany.org
  ChristianServices.org
  CovenantKids.org
  A21.org

Chapter Eighteen
  CancerCenter.com

Chapter Twenty
  PeaceWithGod.net
  NewNameSociety.org
  HopeQuestGlobal.com

MORE ABOUT THE AUTHOR

Gail McWilliams is a seasoned international speaker, multi-published author, and national radio host.

Her courageous and gripping story of gradually losing her eyesight having her children is the backdrop to her life-message of vision that sees no limits.

Gail is an ambassador of hope who has learned to overcome major obstacles with faith and joy. She captivates audiences and inspires them to live life on purpose, with purpose. She is a resilient visionary who inspires action and delivers renewed focus. Gail is intensely challenging and completely unforgettable. Her vivacious personality, effervescent humor, and extraordinary capacity to deliver her life-message are met with broad and energetic approval.

Book Gail Today
For Your Next Event!
888-270-0182
Info@GailMcWilliams.com
www.GailMcWilliams.com